BODY IN THE WAREHOUSE

Readers are encouraged to go to www.MissionPointPress.com to contact the author or to find information on how to buy this book in bulk at a discounted rate.

Published by Mission Point Press
2554 Chandler Lake Rd.
Traverse City, MI 49686
(231) 421-9513
www.MissionPointPress.com

ISBN: 978-1-943995-23-3

Printed in the United States of America.

BODY IN THE WAREHOUSE

A MYSTERY BY
STUART SAFFT

MISSION POINT PRESS

Chapter 1

"**U**h, McFarland," mumbled Joe McFarland, after fumbling around in the dark to locate his cellphone lying on the night table.

"Hello, detective," said the Jasper Creek Police Department dispatcher. "Sorry to wake you, but a body's just been found inside one of the vacant warehouses downtown and you're on call tonight."

"Yeah, I know I'm on call. What time is it?"

"Just past four-thirty, sir."

"And you're still calling this 'tonight'? Jeez! Uh, never mind. What's the address?"

"It's 1220 Melrose, right off Riverside. The body's up on the second floor."

"OK. Call Detective Harris and tell her I'll meet her at the scene in 30 minutes."

"Will do, sir. Good-bye. And, again, I'm sorry."

"I'm sure the dead vic lying in the warehouse is a lot sorrier than you or me. Bye."

And with that, Joe struggled to sit up in bed and turn on the lamp. Rubbing his eyes and then his hair, Joe managed to get up, stagger to the bathroom and begin his abbreviated morning ritual. *I'm getting too old for this middle of the night crap*, Joe told himself. Nonetheless, he was in his car 10 minutes later.

Another 15 minutes and his car was one more official

vehicle parked haphazardly near the front door of the warehouse. The warehouse, a large, three-story, red brick building with vertical metal bars covering all the first floor windows and a heavy wooden front door with peeling brown paint, had clearly seen better days.

Two minutes later Detective Ginny Harris pulled up next to his car and walked over to him.

"Morning, Joe. Lovely time o' day to be meetin' ya."

"How the hell can you be so chipper this time of the morning? There's gotta be something wrong with you."

"Not at all. You have to remember how much younger I am than you."

"Bull. You're a whole four years younger than me."

"Not to belabor the point, but I'm actually four and a half years younger than you. And I also eat and live better than you."

"Well, let's face it, as much as we hate these four a.m. calls, it could be worse. We're both lost souls. No family at home to get pissed off about it, right?"

"Too true. Too true. OK, let's go see what's waiting for us inside."

The patrol officer at the warehouse door immediately recognized Joe and Ginny. "Good morning, detectives," he said, stepping aside as they entered. "Everyone's up on the second floor."

"OK, thanks," both of them replied.

As they stepped out onto the second floor, there was the usual flood of lights and several people standing or walking around the scene, reminding Joe, as crime scenes so often did, of a movie shoot in progress, except no one was acting. There must have been half a dozen Jasper Creek patrolmen, a few securing the interior scene while the others seemed to be just walking around. The crime scene unit was busy examining every inch of the warehouse, collecting all sorts of little nothings in separate plastic bags and dusting everywhere for fingerprints. Two technicians from the coroner's office, as well as the medical examiner himself, were there. There also was one of the assistant prosecutors from the county Prosecutor's Office. Joe and Ginny knew everyone, and nodded back to the quick nods and hellos.

Walking to the right rear corner of the floor, where there was a huge pile of empty boxes and trash, along with one dead body, Joe asked the medical examiner, "Whadda we got, Doc?"

"We'll know more after we autopsy him, but it's a male, probably between 25 and 40 years old. No ID. His wallet is missing. Reasonably well dressed and cared for, so most likely not one of our homeless folks staying in this no-quality, no-cost hotel. Cause of death is almost certainly one or both of the gunshots, one to the head and the other to the chest."

"Jeez. Any idea how long he's been here?" asked Ginny.

"Too early to tell. But, if I had to venture a guess, and I'm sure you two want me to, I'd say somewhere between 12 and 20 hours. I should be able to narrow that down after I get him opened up."

"Think you'll have it in a couple of days?" asked Ginny.

"Should be able to."

"Think he was killed here? Or dumped?" asked Ginny.

"We'll want to see what the crime scene guys come up with, but based upon the blood patterns and the amount of blood, I'm pretty sure he was shot right here."

"Signs of a struggle?" asked Joe.

"Nope. None. No bruises or defensive wounds showing. But we'll know more when we get him downtown."

"He probably knew his killer or the killer was hiding here in all these empty boxes and trash waiting for him," surmised Ginny.

"That'd be my take also," chimed in Joe. "Any idea of the type of gun used?"

"Hard to tell 'til we get him up on the table and remove the slugs. Looks like neither shot was through and through."

"OK, we'll wait to hear from you," responded Ginny.

"OK with you if we remove the body now?" asked the medical examiner.

"Yes. He's all yours," responded Joe.

Less than 10 minutes later, the two technicians had the body tagged and bagged. They lifted it up onto a stretcher, wheeled it to the stairs, and carried it down. The medical examiner followed them out.

Joe walked up to the closest patrol officer. "Who was first on the scene?"

"Jones. He's over there talking with one of the crime scene techs."

"Thanks," said Joe as he and Ginny started walking toward Jones. "Jones, got a minute?" asked Joe.

"Sure, detective."

"We understand that you were first on the scene," said Ginny.

"Yeah, that's right. I was only a few blocks away when the call came in. I was first to arrive, but I stayed outside until two other patrol cars arrived."

"Smart move. Walk us through what happened," said Ginny.

"Well, the call was dispatched right at 3:32 a.m. I was parked out front within five minutes. I checked the front of the building, but I didn't go around back or inside until backup arrived, by which time it was probably 3:45. Schneider and I went inside while Petroni remained out front. We saw nothing unusual on the first floor and then went up the stairs at the front of the building. Sure enough, the vic was lying just where the 9-1-1 caller said he was."

"Who called it in? And where's the caller now?"

"No idea. There was no one here. I haven't heard the 9-1-1 tape, but I was told that it was an anonymous caller."

"Great," said Joe. "An unknown homicide victim, called in by an unknown caller."

"That's perfect for you, Joe," said Ginny with a smile. "Sounds like a case requiring your super-duper detective skills."

Turning back to the patrolman, Ginny asked, "Did you see or hear anything either outside or inside?"

"Not a thing. As you know, it's mostly vacant and derelict buildings around here. A few homeless folks make this area home, but I didn't see or hear anyone this morning. It was dead quiet. No pun intended."

"Gotcha. OK, thanks for your help, Jones. We'll get back to you if we have more questions."

Joe and Ginny spent the next 90 minutes walking

around the crime scene, checking out the first and third floors and handing out assignments to the various patrol officers on the scene.

"Charlie, I know that most of the surrounding buildings are vacant," Joe said to the patrolman he knew was one who got things done quickly and thoroughly. "But not all. There were probably homeless folks in some of them. Start canvassing in a three-block radius. Maybe we'll find someone who saw or heard something. And Bill, follow the same route as Charlie, but focus on trying to locate any video cameras. If we're lucky, we'll have something to look at."

Checking with the crime scene unit confirmed that there were signs of multiple forcible entries, but no way to tell when they occurred. A large number of fingerprints had been found, but it was impossible to tell if they were recent or from months or even years ago. And the only blood found appeared to be the victim's, subject to confirmation in the lab.

"Hey, Joe. Ginny. Got a minute?" bellowed Assistant Prosecutor Ann Messing from the other end of the large warehouse building. Messing was the only woman whom Joe knew whose voice was deeper and louder than his own.

"Yeah! Sure!" yelled Joe in response, a bit sheepish that Messing's voice had been so much louder than his.

Joe and Ginny met Messing as she came their way.

"Hi, Ann," said Ginny. "What brings you out so bright and early?"

"Oh, whenever I can, I like to start my day with an early homicide." Then, as her smile disappeared, she added, "but seriously, this is not pretty. The vic looks like a regular guy, not one of the homeless or druggies, at least on first looks. What was he doing in this part of town? Get us the perp and all the evidence, preferably with a properly Mirandized confession, and we'll race for a quick guilty verdict. That'll keep everyone, including my boss, happy."

"Yeah," said Joe. "And I bet the fact that your boss is running for office again next year has nothing to do with this sense of urgency."

"Well, that might be a minor factor," admitted Messing with a smirk. "But seriously, this case will get a lot of press coverage and political attention, so we all need to march smartly."

"Understood," said Ginny.

"Not to worry," said Joe. "We always march smartly. In fact, we're about to smartly march, or, to be more accurate, smartly drive, to the office right now. We'll be in touch, Ann."

As Joe and Ginny went downstairs and out the door, they were attacked by what seemed to be a dozen TV and newspaper reporters.

"Detectives, what can you tell us? Is it true that …?"

"Hold on," interrupted Joe. "We just started this investigation and have nothing to report at this point."

"But, detect…"

"What part of 'nothing to report' is too complicated for you to understand? I hope I didn't use words that were too big for you."

"Joe, cool it. They're just trying to do their job," whispered Ginny into Joe's ear.

"Detective McFarland and I are heading back to police headquarters. I'm sure you'll be kept informed by PD media relations. Now excuse us please."

Joe and Ginny pushed through the reporters, got into their cars and drove off.

Chapter 2

Arriving back at police headquarters, Joe and Ginny each first grabbed a cup of coffee. Since it was only a little after 7:00 a.m., the coffee wasn't yet as vile as it gets after sitting on the hot plate for hours.

"Whadda ya think, Joe? Any bright ideas or gut feelings yet?"

"Not much, Ginny. I fear that we're going to have to actually work to solve this one. When we get to our desks, we need to first focus on finding out who the vic is and what he was doing in a vacant warehouse in that part of town. Perhaps you can check for missing persons as well as try to light a fire under the fingerprint and DNA folks. While you're getting that started, I'll fill the chief in."

"Sounds like at least the start of a plan."

"Well, every plan needs to start with a start."

"Thanks for explaining that to me, smart ass," said Ginny with a smile.

Ginny headed for her desk to start trying to identify the victim. Joe headed for the chief's office.

Knocking on the door frame around the open door, Joe said, "Good morning, Chief. Got a minute?" and immediately walked in and shut the door without waiting for a response.

"Well, I guess I do, based on you just waltzing in. And why don't you close the door? Oh, excuse me, I see that you already have. Grab a seat. What did you and Ginny find out at that warehouse?"

"Just as advertised: a dead male up on the second floor. No ID but doesn't look like the homeless or druggie type. My gut tells me that this is going to take some work to solve."

"Joe, in the five years you've been here, has your gut ever said anything different at the start of any case?"

"Well, no. But this one is different."

"That's also exactly what you say at the start of every case. So what're your next steps?"

"Ginny and I are focusing on trying to ID the vic. If we can identify him and figure out what he was doing in that abandoned warehouse, we might get a trail to the perp. Ginny's checking with Missing Persons and trying to expedite his fingerprints and DNA analysis. The fingerprints might tell us something fast, but DNA'll take a while."

"Yeah, I know. Any witnesses or sign of his car or surveillance videos or …?"

"So far nothing. We've got the patrol guys running all that down, but I don't hold out much hope. That's a pretty desolate part of town."

"It sure is," said the chief. "And any homeless or druggie who might've seen or heard something will, as usual, be very reluctant to talk to us."

"Tell me something I don't know, Chief. Oh, we're also going to find out who owns that building and go talk with him, but it's a good bet that he knows nothing and isn't involved. And by the way, the media were already all over this outside the warehouse."

"Just what we need. Their reporting will wake up the politicians, who'll start talking their heads off while their heads are up their you-know-where. If you'll pardon the mixed metaphors."

"Fully pardoned, Chief. Well, that's the scoop. Let me get back out there and give Ginny a hand. We'll keep you informed as things develop."

"Thanks, Joe. And good luck."

And with that, Joe was out the door and back at his desk opposite Ginny.

Chapter 3

"**G**inny, can you please put your magical computer skills to work again? Let's find out who owns that dump of a building and go pay him a visit," said Joe.

"Sure thing. Just give me a couple of minutes to finish this, then I'll get a name from Property Records' database."

"OK."

Ten minutes later, Ginny was back from the printer. "OK, I got a name for us. The building is owned by a small, local real estate firm, JC Realty Investments Ltd. The owner and president is a Theodore Pentell and their offices are only a few blocks from here. Pentell has no priors and isn't in the system."

"That's fine," replied Joe. "But we don't know whether that means he's honest or he's good at his criminal activities."

"Should I call and make an appointment?"

"No. Let's just walk over there now. I prefer not pre-announcing our visit and giving him time to think up all types of brilliant bullshit before we get to talk to him."

"Oh, ye of little faith. But I'm with you in this case."

Less than 10 minutes later, Joe and Ginny were riding the elevator up to the fourth floor, which is where the directory in the lobby indicated that JC Realty Investments' headquarters was. Opening the door, they quickly realized that "headquarters" was a bit of an exaggeration.

Rather, there was a small reception area with a pretty but very young receptionist sitting behind a gray metal desk. There was one door in the rear corner, no doubt leading to the "executive offices" of Theodore Pentell.

"Good morning," said Ginny to the receptionist. "We'd like to see Mr. Pentell."

"Oh. Oh, OK. Do you have an appointment? What are your names?"

"No, we don't have an appointment. I'm Detective Harris and this is Detective McFarland. We're with the Jasper Creek Police Department."

"Oh my goodness. Is everything all right?"

"We're just here to speak with Mr. Pentell."

"I'm sorry but he's not here." Before Joe could jump in and call her a liar who could be charged with impeding a criminal investigation, the receptionist continued, "But I expect him to arrive any minute now."

"OK. Thank you," replied Ginny. "We'll just sit over there and wait."

Sure enough, five minutes later, a balding man in his mid-40s entered. Before he could even close the door, Joe was up and right in front of him. "Mr. Pentell? Mr. Theodore Pentell?"

"Yes. And who are you?"

"Jasper Creek Police Department. I'm Detective Harris and this is Detective McFarland," said Ginny as she walked up to them.

"Is there a problem?" Are my wife and children all right?"

"Yes, as far as we know. We'd like to talk with you about a different matter."

"Yes, sure. Please come into my office. Would you like some coffee?"

"No. But thank you," answered Ginny for Joe and herself.

Inside the office, Pentell sat in his chair, behind another gray metal desk, but one larger than that of the receptionist. Joe and Ginny sat in the two small chairs facing the desk.

"Yes?" asked Pentell.

"Do you own the vacant warehouse at 1220 Melrose?" asked Joe without any preamble.

"Well, yes, sort of."

"Please, don't start getting evasive already," said Joe in his often-antagonistic manner. "What is that supposed to mean?"

"I'm not being evasive. I was going to explain. Technically my corporation, JC Realty Investments Ltd., owns that building. And I own JC Realty Investments Ltd. So that's why I answered 'sort of.' "

"OK," responded Joe. "Do you know what took place there this morning?"

"What? No. What happened? That building's been totally vacant for almost five years. Not another break-in. Damn."

"Detective Harris and I spent a good part of last night and this morning there. A body was found on the second floor."

"Oh, my god. That's horrible! Please believe me, we try to keep the homeless and the drug addicts out as best we can, but they're always breaking in or going around whatever locks we install. To think, an overdose death in one of our buildings. Is there anything I should do?"

"Slow down, Mr. Pentell," said Ginny. "The person didn't die of an overdose."

"Oh, what was it then? It wasn't cold enough to freeze to death last night."

"No, it wasn't," agreed Ginny. "We're waiting for the medical examiner to complete his evaluation, but we fully expect him to conclude that the victim was shot to death."

"Oh, my goodness. How could that be?"

"Mr. Pentell, please take a look at this photo of the victim. Do you know him? Have you seen him before?"

"No. No. I don't think so. I don't know him and don't think I've ever seen him. In fact, I haven't even been in that building for almost a year. It's been that long since we've had a prospective buyer or lessee wanting to see the building."

"Mr. Pentell, can you tell us a bit about the history of the building and your, or, I should say, your firm's ownership of it?"

"Sure. The history is pretty straightforward. My father, may he rest in peace, owned the building, along with three other buildings in that part of town, for probably 35 or maybe even 40 years. By the time he was getting ready to retire five or six years ago, I already had JC Realty Investments set up, although it only owned a couple of small properties back then. I started the company soon after my discharge from the Army when I returned to Jasper Creek. My company purchased this and the other buildings from my father when he was ready to retire."

"Interesting," said Joe. "Where did you serve? I spent almost a year with the Army in the late '90s in Bosnia."

"I was in the Army from 1998 to 2006. After basic training, I was sent to Germany and spent my entire tour there, basically doing nothing of any value. Anyhow, while my father owned the building and even for a few years after that, it was fully rented out. The tenants changed every few years, but the building never was less than fully rented for more than a few months at a time. The tenants were all light manufacturing companies, some with pieces of equipment like drills and small presses, but most were basic assembly operations. Then, as I'm sure you're well aware, more and more of our manufacturing moved, first to the south and then to Asia. And, as a result, the building has been vacant for about four years. And there've been very few potential tenants, none of which panned out."

"Why didn't you sell the building?" asked Ginny.

"I'd love to. But there's been no one interested, except for a few bums trying to buy it for pennies on the dollar. Periodically, the government talks about buying a bunch of properties in the area and stimulating redevelopment by putting one or more of their operations there, but these government plans never seem to pan out. So here we are, still owning it, paying property taxes, insurance and a little maintenance, and trying best we can to keep the homeless and drug addicts out of the building. And all this with zero rental income."

"So what will happen with the building?" Ginny asked.

"Nothing, until, or unless, sometime in the future, the

economy improves, firms start manufacturing again in the U.S. and that whole section of town picks back up. Or some government agency truly decides to convert these buildings to government offices as way to jump-start the whole area."

"Mr. Pentell, can you tell us where you were yesterday, all day and into the evening?"

"Whoa! What? Am I a suspect?"

"No, not at all. We don't have any suspects yet. This is just a routine question that we ask. If nothing else, it helps us cross folks off the possible-suspect list," replied Ginny.

"Well, it so happens I have what I think you will admit is a good so-called alibi. As if I need one. From about 10 a.m. until almost five, I was in meetings, either in person or by phone. I can give you a list of who I met with. Then from about 5:15 to almost seven, I was having dinner with one of my attorneys, Bill Simmons, at Chez Rose around the corner. Then he and I spent from about 7:15 until almost 10 p.m.at the Planning & Zoning Commission meeting in City Hall. We were busy dealing with all the BS bureaucracy surrounding our request for a zoning variance for another building we own on the other side of town. I'm sure that many who were there can confirm this for you. After the meeting, Bill and I grabbed a quick drink around the corner from City Hall and then I went home and went to bed."

"Can anyone vouch for when you got home?" asked Joe.

"Uh, no. I live alone. My wife and I are separated."

"Well, thank you for that information about your

whereabouts yesterday. Yes, the list of whom you had meetings with, along with their phone numbers, would be useful."

Pentell spent the next 10 minutes repeatedly checking his calendar and writing down the names and phone numbers of everyone he met with or spoke with the day before. He gave the list to Ginny when he had finished.

"And thank you for your time, Mr. Pentell," replied Ginny. "We may be back if we have more questions. Here's my card. Please call if you think of anything."

"I will. But I doubt if I'll think of anything."

And five minutes later, Joe and Ginny were out of the office, down the elevator and on the sidewalk heading back to PD headquarters.

"Well, that was a total waste of time," said Joe.

"We knew it probably would be, but we had to check it out. At least we had a nice little walk in the fresh air."

"Yeah. And it helped us probably eliminate one suspect. It's unlikely Pentell had anything to do with the killing."

"Agreed," said Ginny just as they were entering the PD. "But I'll run down the list he gave us just to be sure his alibi's solid."

"That's what any top-notch detective would do," said Joe with a smile.

Chapter 4

Their coffee cups refilled, Joe and Ginny were back sitting at their desks facing each other.

"I'll write up our notes from this morning, while you focus on trying to identify our vic," offered Joe.

"That's what I was already starting to do before you invited me on our field trip to Pentell's office."

Joe took his notepad out of his pocket and opened it. Putting a clean sheet of paper into his ancient manual typewriter, he focused his attention on typing a legible version of his terse notes, adding details that he remembered as he typed. Ginny, using her computer, searched the missing-persons files for Jasper Creek and every other jurisdiction in the area.

After about 45 minutes, Ginny swiveled her chair toward Joe and said, "There's nothing in the missing-persons files. No one reported missing within 100 miles of here even remotely resembles our vic. Most are teenagers who seem to have run away or seniors who have wandered off."

"I'm not surprised. It's still pretty soon after the estimated time of death. Either he's not even been noticed as missing yet, or whichever town got the call hasn't yet entered it into the system."

"Well, I've flagged all the systems to send us a notification if someone resembling our guy is added to the database."

"That's all you can do on that score for now. I'm going to check to see whether we lucked out on any witnesses or surveillance videos in the area."

"OK, Joe. And I'm going to mosey down to Finger-printing to see where they are and, if need be, light a little fire under their butts."

"Good idea, Ginny. See you back here in a bit."

Twenty minutes later, Joe and Ginny were back at their desks.

"Nothing in terms of videos," said Joe. "Also no witnesses. I'm not surprised about the lack of cameras in that neighborhood, but I'm sure there were some druggies and homeless in that area and someone had to have seen or heard something."

"For sure. But these folks are as likely to talk to us as they are to talk to the pope," Ginny said. "When's the last time we — or anyone working for the city — did them any favors? The good thing is that they don't *all* hate us. Some are just afraid of us."

"And I for one don't blame them," Joe replied. "But we have to try, right? Maybe someone who saw something might just be willing to tell us. Worth a try. We'll see. I asked the patrol guys to go back out to find some of these folks and gently interview them, even bribing them with a few bucks if they think it might help get them to open up."

"Can't hurt to try. Meanwhile, they're still checking all the fingerprints in our local files as well as the Feebie's IAFIS database. It'll be another hour or so before they have any results."

"OK. Let's get some of the damn paperwork on some of our other cases out of the way while we're waiting. Then we can check back with them after lunch."

"Sounds like you have a plan again," replied Ginny. "But before I get back to that, I want to call the names Pentell gave us."

About 20 minutes later, Ginny hung up her phone and turned to Joe. "Well, Joe, as we suspected, Pentell's alibi's rock-solid. At least we've confirmed one non-suspect. At least for now."

"Yeah, we didn't get much from Pentell that seems helpful at this point, but crossing him off the suspect list is something."

A few minutes before noon, Joe and Ginny began their lunch-routine dance. Virtually every day that they were in or near police headquarters when lunchtime rolled around, they had their ritual debate.

"Joe, let's go get Chinese for a change. It's been quite a while."

"I was really thinking of pizza — all meat, of course. Although, just for you, I'd be agreeable to have the pizza damaged by burying half of it under a pile of different veggies."

"Boy, we sure have a tough time agreeing on important issues, like where to have lunch."

"Yes, we do."

"I hate to say it, Joe, but we must sound like an old married couple."

"Yeah, well, if this is the biggest disagreement we ever have, I think we're in pretty good shape."

"Agreed. And, in order to maintain our marital, not to mention partnering bliss, let's once again head over to Sancho's."

"That's a deal," said Joe as they walked around the corner and settled in at the local taco shop.

While munching on their burritos and tacos, one of each for each of them, Ginny reflected on how much she had enjoyed partnering with Joe these past three and a half years. Although Joe was extremely gruff, and sometimes crude on the outside, Ginny had come to recognize a softer, more caring and sensitive person buried deep within him. She attributed his gruff exterior to the defense mechanism he put in place to avoid getting too close to or, heaven forbid, dependent on anyone else. This, she was sure, was because his wife and young son were killed by a drunk driver 11 years earlier while he was with the Chicago Police Department. Ginny continued to feel herself getting drawn closer to Joe on a personal, not just professional, basis. She again resolved to keep these feelings controlled and hidden as she feared complete rejection by Joe if she were to voice or act upon her feelings. For the moment, she was content with their close working relationship and friendship.

From his standpoint, Joe was just relieved that he hadn't blushed or otherwise reacted to Ginny's marital quips. Joe had not yet figured out how to cope with, much less express, his growing affection for Ginny.

Back from their quick lunch, Ginny went directly to the fingerprint and DNA lab.

"Hiya, Bill. Any results for me yet?"

"Yes and no, Ginny. We've got results from our finger-print searches, but the DNA will take a while longer."

"Yeah, that's what I expected. So whadda ya have?"

"I won't have the full report ready until tomorrow morning, but here's what we have. As you know, there was a shit pile of fingerprints throughout the warehouse. And there's no way to tell which, if any, were fresh and which were months or years old. Of the 37 different sets of full or partial prints, we've identified 11 individuals from our local files and 17 others from the FBI's database. I'll have files on all of these folks to you by the end of today."

"Great. Do any of them jump out as likely suspects?"

"Quite honestly, I've been so busy capturing, cleaning and submitting these fingerprints that I haven't even looked at the reports yet. If we'd ever upgrade our finger-printing system to the digital systems now used through-out most of the civilized world, I could have done this in half the time."

"Tell me about it. I remain shocked that we don't still have rotary phones. The chief is so proud that our pencils have erasers on one end. That to him is hi-tech."

"I know exactly what you mean."

"Bill, how about the fingerprints from the vic? It would really kick-start our investigation if we could identify him."

"Well then, I've got good news for you."

"And?"

"We got a match from IAFIS. Your vic is Paul Dalton."

"Great! What's his rap sheet say?"

"Nothing. There is no rap sheet. His prints were in IAFIS because he's former military, not a criminal."

"Oh, bad assumption on my part. Let me have whatever you have on him, and I'll get out of your hair."

Rummaging through a stack of paper on his desk, Bill found the sheet and handed it to Ginny. "Here you go. Here's what we've got. I'll also include a copy of this in the written report."

"OK. And thanks, Bill."

"Don't mention it. That's what we're here for."

Ginny hurried back to her desk, skimming the report on her way.

Once seated at her desk, she jumped right in. "Joe, we got an ID on the vic."

"Super. Who is he?"

"His name is Paul Dalton."

"And?"

"Not much for us to grab onto. No criminal record. His address is shown as Kansas City. That's Kansas City, Missouri, not Kansas City, Kansas. Owns a 2010 Honda Civic, with Missouri plates."

"OK, that's a start. Why don't you see what else you can find out about him?"

"Will do. Gimme a few minutes."

As promised, 15 minutes later Ginny had some additional information.

"Joe, here's what else I was able to find out about Dalton. He was born outside Kansas City in 1977 and lived there until he went off to college. His father was an auto mechanic and his mother was a saleslady in one of the local department stores. Nothing out of the ordinary reported. After high school, Dalton went to Missouri State University in Springfield. After graduating, he married his high school sweetheart, and then joined the Army. He was stationed at Fort Bragg, N.C. where he and his wife lived on the base. He had several overseas assignments, but I couldn't get any details. Left the Army in 2009 and he and his wife returned to Kansas City. They had a baby daughter soon after that. His current address is still shown as the one in Kansas City."

"Jeez, it sure puts things in perspective sometimes."

"What do you mean?"

"He's only a few years younger than me and only a year or so older than you. He coulda been my friend or your husband."

"Yeah, right. But he isn't either. Now he's just our vic."

"And now we have some work to do."

"I'll call the Kansas City police and arrange for them to inform the widow of her husband's death. I'll also start the wheels in motion for us to interview her. I hope she's able to come here to identify and claim the body. Otherwise, we'll have to make the big trip to KC. If we do wind up out there, we can talk to some of his high school and college friends or teachers. Both his parents are dead."

"OK. And, Ginny, don't forget all the great Kansas City BBQ we can pig out on."

"Good thing you mentioned that, Joe. Wouldn't have wanted to forget the most important reason for the trip."

"That's what makes us such a great team. I'm always there to correct your errors."

"Gee, thanks, partner. It's amazing I can put my shoes on in the morning without your help."

"Feel free to give me a call whenever you need help with your shoes. In the meantime, while you're contacting the KC PD, I'll try to get some more details on his Army service and his time at Fort Bragg."

Ginny had a short phone call with the Kansas City police. They promised to send a patrol car to the Dalton residence to deliver the news of her husband's death to Mrs. Dalton. They also agreed to conduct a preliminary interview with her to see whether she had any useful information and to ask whether she'd be going to Ohio to identify and reclaim her husband's body. Ginny thanked the officer and said she'd wait to hear back from him later that same day.

Joe's efforts with the U.S. Army weren't nearly as productive. After getting shuffled from office to office and officer to officer, he finally was connected to the Fort Bragg Public Affairs Office.

"Good afternoon. This is Lieutenant Jensen with the Public Affairs Office at Fort Bragg, home of the U.S. Army's Airborne and Special Operations Forces. How may I help you?"

"Good afternoon, Lieutenant. I'm Detective Joe McFarland with the Jasper Creek Police Department here in southeast Ohio."

"Good afternoon, Sir. What can we do for you?"

"I'm calling to get some information about a former soldier who was stationed at Fort Bragg."

"If you'll give me his name and the years of his service, and what type of information you're looking for, I'll see what I can do."

"Great. His name is Paul Dalton, that's D-A-L-T-O-N, and I believe he was in the Army from sometime in 2000 until sometime in 2009, with all or much of that time, except for some overseas assignments, at Fort Bragg."

"And what information are you looking for?"

"I'd like to get as much of his personnel folder as possible. Specifically, his various assignments, his superiors, names of others he worked with, any discipline or mental issues and so on."

"I'm sorry, sir, but it may turn out that much of that can't be released. If that proves to be the case, other than some very basic info, you'll need a warrant to get more, and even then, much of the info may not be released for national security reasons."

"Mr. Dalton was found dead this morning and we'd like to find his killer or killers. And I assume that the U.S. Army would like to help us all they can in this effort."

"Yes, sir, we would. Awfully sorry to hear about his murder. And you think it's related to his Army service?"

"No idea. That's what we're trying to find out."

"Yes, sir. Hold on a minute. Let me look up his records on the computer and tell you all that I can. This may take four or five minutes."

"No problem. I can wait, Lieutenant."

Five minutes later, Lieutenant Jensen was back on the phone. "Hello, detective. Are you still there?"

"Yes I am. Whadda ya got?"

"I'm afraid that my hunch was correct. Almost all of the information is classified and can't be released."

"What *can* you tell me?"

"Well, I can confirm that he was on active duty, as you said, from 2000 to 2009, and that he was assigned to Fort

Bragg for much of that period. In fact, he and his wife lived in base housing a good part of that time. Except for the early part of his career, he was in Special Ops, but none of those details can be released."

"Can you put me in touch with his commanding officer?'

"No, sir. That's part of the confidential information. You may be able to get more information if you put your specific information requests in writing to us. But, I have to warn you, it takes quite a while for letters like that to work their way up the command chain."

"Jeez, that's not gonna help. We're trying to solve a homicide here. Do I get any slack because I'm also ex-Army?"

"Fraid not, sir. But that at least makes you familiar with the rules and the bureaucracy of the Army."

"Yeah, only too well. I know that you're just following the rules."

"Thank you, sir. And good luck with your investigation. Hope you find the bastard that did this."

"We will. Thanks and good-bye."

Joe turned back to his desk and filled Ginny in on his waste of time talking with the Army. Just as he was finishing, Ginny's phone rang.

"Hi, detective. This is Sergeant James from Kansas City. Wanted to let you know that our officers made contact with Mrs. Dalton and gave her the bad news."

Ginny put her phone on speaker so that Joe could hear both sides of the conversation. "Thanks for the quick follow-up, Sergeant. Any details worth repeating?"

"Well, it turns out that she wasn't all that broken up

about it. Seems that their marriage went south pretty soon after he left the Army. She said he became very moody and depressed, maybe even paranoid. They haven't been living together for the past nine months. She hasn't seen nor spoken with him, nor gotten any money from him. Not even any money for their daughter. If it weren't for her parents helping out, she'd probably be on welfare by now."

"Jeez, that's a shame. But we hear that all too often with military families."

"Yeah, so do we. He apparently went to the local VA hospital for help, but it didn't do much good. They gave him some meds and made him an appointment for six months out. She said that the meds made him feel so tired and goofy that he just stopped taking them."

"Unfortunately, we also hear stories like that all the time."

"Tell me about it. In any event, the wife, or I guess I should say the widow, doesn't have the funds or the interest to come east. She will take care of the funeral, but would like the body shipped to Kansas City. She said she'd pay for that."

"OK, we'll let you know when the medical examiner finishes his work and releases the body. Looks like my partner and I will be coming out to your neck of the woods, if you don't mind."

"Not a problem. Happy to help. In fact, let me know when you're set and I'll have one of our officers pick you up at the airport. And it will be my pleasure to introduce both of you to the dang best BBQ in the whole U.S."

"Great. And many thanks. We'll get back to you, most

likely later today, once we have our trip arranged. So long for now."

"Bye."

"Well, Ginny, looks like we're off to KC. Let's fill in the chief and get his OK for the trip. Then it's way past time to head home."

"I agree with that, especially since we started this day in the middle of the night."

And so Joe and Ginny brought the chief up to date and got his reluctant approval for their trip. Ginny checked for flights, made flight and hotel reservations for Joe and herself and called Sergeant James of the Kansas City PD to inform him of their travel plans. He confirmed that he would have one of his officers pick them up when they arrived at the airport.

Chapter 5

At 7:00 the next morning, Joe and Ginny met at Gate 23 at Cincinnati/Northern Kentucky International Airport. The nonstop Delta flight left a mere 10 minutes late, and, two hours later, Joe and Ginny were walking off the plane into the Kansas City Airport.

As they exited through the security area, they saw a uniformed Kansas City patrolman standing there and looking at each arriving passenger. Joe walked up to him and asked, "Are you waiting for Detectives McFarland and Harris?"

"Well, yes I am. Was it that obvious?"

"We knew that an officer was going to meet us, and you're the only one dressed appropriately. I'm Joe McFarland and this is Detective Ginny Harris. Thanks for meeting us."

"No problem. That's what the Sarge told me to do, so that's what I do. I'm Bob Jakowski."

"Nice to meet you, Bob," said Ginny, as she shook his hand.

"Likewise."

Having only carry-on luggage, Ginny and Joe followed Officer Jakowski right to his patrol car parked in front of the terminal.

"I'm yours for the duration of your visit. Where'd you

like to go to first? Police headquarters? Your hotel? The widow?"

"Let's head over and talk with the widow first," answered Ginny.

"Sure, no problem. It'll probably take us about a half-hour to get there. Hop in. Joe, given the length of your legs vs. Ginny's, I suggest you ride up front."

"Works for me. Ginny, you OK with that?"

"Sure, Daddy Long Legs," answered Ginny.

Just about 30 minutes later, they pulled up in front of a small, single-story, bungalow-style house. A light blue, vinyl-siding front, with white trim around the windows and doors, made the house look more like a beach bungalow than a house in the Midwest. The front yard was quite small, yet the advancing weeds seemed to be rapidly overtaking the grass. There were a few small red azalea bushes against the front of the house; they appeared not to have been trimmed for at least a year.

"I'll come in with you," said Jakowski, "but just to lend some local authority. After introductions, I'll leave the questioning up to you."

"Thanks, Bob," said Joe.

They walked up the short walk to the front door and Jakowski rang the bell. They heard a child crying, then the mother's harsh words, meant to be whispered, but they carried through the closed door. A minute later, the door opened.

"Yes?" asked Kristi Dalton.

She clearly was an attractive woman, despite her current frazzled look and housekeeping-like outfit. About five-feet-eight, thin but not skinny. Short, dirty blond hair encircled a long, thin face, highlighted by blue-gray eyes and a perfectly straight nose.

"Good morning, ma'am," said Jakowski. "Are you Mrs. Dalton?"

"Yes, I am."

"May we come in and speak with you, ma'am? I'm Officer Jakowski with the KC PD. These here are Detectives McFarland and Harris from Ohio. They'd like to speak with you about your husband."

"Yes, sure. Please come in. Sorry about the mess, but I've been busy caring for the little one. She's got a cold and it's making her miserable. I was planning to straighten up later today."

"That's not a problem, Mrs. Dalton. We understand," said Ginny.

Mrs. Dalton led them all into a small living room near the rear of the house. She removed the newspaper from one chair and toys from the couch and invited them to sit down. "Would you like some coffee?"

"No, thanks," responded Joe. "We've been guzzling coffee since early this morning. I don't think I could manage even one more sip."

"OK. I suppose you want to ask me some questions about Paul. Can you please first tell me whatever you can about how he died?"

"Well, we don't have many facts yet, but it appears that he was killed, shot to death," said Ginny. "His body was found in a deserted warehouse. We, and the medical examiner, are just starting our investigation so we don't yet know very much at all about the who and whys of the case. We're hoping that our talk with you will help us in our investigation."

"Oh, my god. What a terrible thing. And what a terrible way to die. Was it a robbery or something like that?"

"As we said, Mrs. Dalton, we don't have much to go on yet. That's why we'd like to get some information from you," said Ginny.

"I understand. I'm sure you'd rather switch to where you're asking me the questions."

"Yes, that's correct, Mrs. Dalton. Let me start by saying how very sorry we are for your loss," said Ginny.

"Please, call me 'Kristi.' Whenever I hear 'Mrs. Dalton,' I still think of Paul's mother, may she rest in peace. And thank you for your comment, but the sad truth is that I lost Paul a couple of years ago."

"What do you mean?" asked Joe.

"Paul and I were in love all through high school and while he was in college. We got married right after he graduated. Within a few months, he joined the Army. That was something he had talked about for years, and I was fine with it. Paul was a true, old-fashioned patriot and he wanted to do his part to protect the country and, as he would put it, our way of life."

"Good for him," said Joe.

"Well, one thing led to another," continued Kristi, "and Paul wound up in Special Operations. We even lived on the base at Fort Bragg for a while."

"His being in Special Operations must have been hard on you," volunteered Ginny.

"Yes it was. Very. But it was what made Paul happy, so I

learned to live with it. And I was very proud of him. The hardest part was all the times he was away on missions. He couldn't tell me where he was going or how long he'd be away. Every time the phone or doorbell rang, I durn near had a heart attack, thinking it was some officers to tell me that he'd been injured or captured or killed."

"That had to be a scary way to live," said Ginny.

"Yes, it was. But whenever he returned home, things were great. We managed through it for almost seven years, and then Paul finally agreed to leave the service."

"When was that?" asked Joe.

"April of 2009. We were so happy to be back together. We immediately moved back here to Kansas City, and our daughter was born nine months later."

"Sounds good. What did Joe do for a living after the Army?" asked Joe.

"That's when the problems began. He worked at just about everything and nothing. He tried a number of things, and many folks gave him a chance. We knew many of them and others just wanted to lend a hand to an ex-serviceman, but he couldn't stick with anything for more than a month or two."

"That's too bad. What was going on?" asked Ginny.

"It had to have been some of the stuff he saw, or did, on those Special Ops assignments. But he never talked about it. At least not with me. Once he left the service, he quickly became very moody and depressed. He wound up with a terrible temper, which he never had before. He basically crawled into a shell and closed it behind himself. No one, not even I, could reach him. He didn't want to do anything, or go out, or be with most other people. He was only comfortable when he occasionally was with other former Special Ops guys."

"Did he get any help from the military?" asked Joe.

"You gotta be kidding. He went to the local VA hospital for help. One visit and they loaded him up with antidepressant and tranquilizer prescriptions. The meds were making him feel so tired and goofy that he just stopped taking them after a few weeks. He called the VA and they gave him an appointment. For six months out! Can you believe it? Six months out! He never bothered going back."

"What a damn shame," said Joe.

"Then about nine months ago, I was out food shopping with our daughter. When I got home, Paul was gone. He took a small amount of cash and a few changes of clothing, and that was it."

"How'd you know that he voluntarily left and that something hadn't happened to him?" asked Joe.

"Oh, he was kind enough to leave me a note. I can quote exactly what it said: 'Sorry, Kristi, but I can't do this. Bye. Love, Paul.' "

"Wow, talk about short and sweet," said Joe.

"Are you kidding?" asked Kristi. "That's the most communications we'd had in about a year."

"What's happened between you and Paul since he left?" asked Ginny.

"Nothing. I haven't seen or spoken with him, or gotten any money from him, in almost nine months. Not even any money for our daughter. Until the police called about his death, I had no idea where he was. I surely wouldn't have guessed Ohio."

"Any idea when or why he went to Ohio? Does he have any friends or relatives there? Had he been there previously?" asked Ginny.

"I have no idea why. I know that he doesn't have relatives there. In fact, both his parents have been dead for a number of years. He was an only child, and we never saw or even spoke with any of his cousins. It's possible that he knew someone from Special Ops who's in Ohio. He had several Army buddies that he was close to on assignments, but not really anyone I can think of who lived in Ohio. We tended to not mix very much socially when he was in the service. We pretty much stayed by ourselves and did our own thing. I was friendly with several of the other wives when we lived on the base, for the times when our husbands were away, but I don't recall any of them being from Ohio."

"It would help if you could give us the names, and contact information if you have it, for any of the soldiers or wives that Paul and you were friendly with," said Ginny as she handed Kristi her pad and pen.

Kristi wrote down a few names and addresses, and included a couple phone numbers. She then went into the kitchen and came back with a black-covered, well-worn address book. She spent about 10 minutes going through the book and, every so often, copied an entry onto the note paper.

"That's about the only ones I can think of," said Kristi. "As I said before, Paul had some other friends from the service but I either never met them or only met them long enough to say 'hello' and 'good-bye.' "

"Don't worry about it," said Ginny. "What you gave us should provide a good starting point."

"Any pictures of your husband with some of his Army buddies?" asked Joe.

"Not a one," answered Kristi. "Paul ripped them all up and threw them away one day in one of his fits of anger."

"What a shame," said Joe.

"Have you checked with some of these people on the list to try and learn any more about why Paul left and what he's been doing?" asked Ginny.

"I've tried, but I couldn't reach many of them. I'm still in fairly close contact with Mary Cook. She doesn't live far from here. And I've spoken with Ed Snyder, one of Paul's military buddies, and Matt Hardy, another of his Army friends who lives in Texas. But none of them knew anything."

"What about the others on the list?" asked Ginny.

"I don't have the phone numbers or addresses for a couple of them. And one of them, Alan Meyers, who had been Paul's best friend from about fourth grade, I called twice and left messages both times, but he never called me back. Soon after my second call, he just showed up here one evening. He said he knew nothing about what had changed Paul. He spent most of the hour or so he was here trying to make me feel better about my situation and encouraging me to remain positive and hopeful. I appreciated what Alan was trying to do, but it didn't really help much as he knew nothing specific he could tell me."

"That's too bad," concluded Ginny.

The three of them then talked through the procedures, paperwork and estimated timing for getting Paul's body shipped back home. Joe and Ginny promised to call Kristi as soon as the medical examiner was ready to release the body. They gave Kristi their business cards, thanked her again and repeated their condolences. Joe, Ginny and Jakowski were then out the door and back in the patrol car.

Chapter 6

Ginny studied the list that Kristi had given her. "There are seven people on this list. Three are around here, three are at Fort Bragg and one has a Texas address. We'd like to try to see the three local ones today and tomorrow morning," she said to Jakowski. "I'm not sure if Sergeant James told you, but we're on a flight back to Ohio tomorrow at about two in the afternoon. While we're here, we'd also like to visit his high school and college and talk with the principal or dean; they may have more info about him or his friends."

"And we'd also like to swing by the local Army recruiting station where Paul enlisted. Hopefully, someone will have some useful tidbits of info for us," said Joe.

"OK. Let me see the list you have. Gimme a couple of minutes to check out all the addresses, then I can come up with a halfway logical route and sequence of people to see," said Jakowski. "For his college, I think you might want to start with a phone call rather than a visit. Missouri State is in Springfield, and that's about a three-hour drive each way."

"Oh, then we're definitely in favor of phoning rather than visiting the college. At least as a first step," said Ginny.

Their next stop was only a few miles away. On the way, they stopped at a Burger King for a fast lunch. A Whopper for Ginny and Double Whoppers for the two men, with large fries and Diet Cokes for all. They got their food and woofed it down in all of 15 minutes before climbing back into the patrol car and on to their next interview.

Mary and Shaun Cook had gone to high school with Paul and Kristi and stayed close friends for years. In fact, Shaun had joined the Navy at about the same time that Paul had joined the Army. Except for the time the Daltons were living at Fort Bragg, Kristi and Mary were best friends, especially as both of their husbands were away from home so often. Pulling up to their apartment house, Jakowski led the way to apartment 206. When Mary answered the door, Jakowski introduced himself and the two Jasper Creek detectives and then stepped into the background. The questioning took only a few minutes. Mary explained that although she and Kristi still remained fairly close, her husband and Paul had drifted apart. Shaun was working full-time as the assistant manager of a local branch of a large regional bank.

"Ever since Paul and Kristi returned from Fort Bragg, Paul no longer seemed the same person he had been," Mary said. "It was probably the result of his time in Special Operations. He became bitter, introverted and depressed. Shaun at first tried to reason with him and tried to get him to seek medical help more aggressively, but it didn't seem to help. Shaun hasn't seen or spoken with Paul for about two and a half years."

"And have you remained close to Kristi?" asked Ginny.

"Not as close as we were years ago, but still pretty close. I've tried to be there for her ever since Paul left. It's been real hard for her."

"Do you have any idea where Paul went after he left Kristi?" asked Joe.

"No, I don't. I assume he's somewhere in the area, but I really don't know."

Ginny and Joe thanked Mary for her time, gave her their business cards and headed back to the car.

"Where to next?" asked Joe.

"Let's head over to the high school that Paul went to. It's close by."

"OK. Go for it, Bob," Joe replied.

A few minutes later they arrived at the school, made their introductions and were led right into the principal's office.

"Hello. I'm John Rohr. I've been the principal here for the past 21 years. What can I help you with?"

"We're trying to gather some background information on a Paul Dalton. He went here and graduated in 1995," said Joe.

"That name sounds vaguely familiar. But an awful lot of students have passed through here over the years. Give me a couple of minutes." Rohr stepped out of his office and soon returned with a yearbook and a manila folder in his hand. "Let me just take a quick look here and refresh my memory."

"Sure. Take your time," said Joe.

After a few minutes of searching through the yearbook and skimming the file, Rohr said "Oh, yes. I remember Paul. A very nice boy. A good student. Not brilliant, but he applied himself and got decent grades. Went onto college right after he graduated."

Joe replied, "He apparently then married his high school

sweetheart, a Kristi Johnson, after which he joined the Army. He's been out about three years now. He recently left his wife and has sort of gone missing. Any idea where he might have gone?"

"Uh, no. No idea at all. I don't think I've seen him, or even thought about him, since his high school days."

"Anything unusual about his activities or friends while he was in school here?"

"No, I don't think so. I can't recall anything unusual and there's nothing indicated in his file."

"OK. Thank you for your time, Mr. Rohr. May we borrow that yearbook for a day or two? We'd like to browse through it and see if it gives us any more insight into his high school years. Sports, clubs, friends. That sort of thing."

"You're quite welcome. I just wish I could have been of more help. Sure, here's the yearbook," he said as he handed it to Joe.

"Thanks. We'll be heading back to Ohio, but Officer Jakowski here will see to it that this is returned to you," said Joe.

"OK, that'll be fine."

They spent the next several minutes sitting in the car while Ginny called Paul's college, Missouri State University. They had equally unhelpful telephone discussions with the dean of students and the dean of admissions, neither of whom had even been at the college during the years that Paul attended. They did at least arrange for the dean of students to send a copy of the yearbook for the year of Paul's graduation to Ginny in Jasper Creek. Ginny promised to send it back within a few days of receiving it.

"Well at least we did this by phone rather than driving for three hours to see them in person," said Ginny.

Next they drove to downtown Kansas City, Kansas, to check with the Army recruiting station. During the trip, Ginny went through the high school yearbook and made a list of pages of interest. She left the book and page numbers so that Jakowski could photocopy the selected pages and mail them to Ginny, and return the yearbook to the principal.

Jakowski parked right in front, and the three of them walked into the storefront recruiting station.

"Good afternoon, lady and gentlemen. How can I help you? I'm Corporal Dolores Ford. You three don't look like you're ready to enlist."

"Very perceptive, Corporal," Joe said. "In fact, I've already served, including a tour in Bosnia."

"Good for you, Sir. How can I help you?"

I'm Detective McFarland and this is Detective Harris. We're with the Jasper Creek, Ohio, police force."

"And I'm Officer Jakowski with the KC, Missouri, PD."

"All the way from Ohio. This must be important."

"It is. We'd like to get some information on a Paul Dalton. He enlisted back in 2000, and we're assuming through this recruiting station," said Joe.

"Let me check. Luckily, we completed converting the old paper files all the way back to 1985 to the computer about two years ago. So if he did enlist here in 2000, it should be in the computer database. Just give me a couple of minutes." Corporal Ford turned to her keyboard and computer screen, moving the mouse and pressing keys.

"Oh, here he is. Yes, 2000 is correct. April 6th to be exact."

"What info is in the record?" asked Ginny.

"Well, it has things like his address at that time, his social security number, who to call in case of an emergency and so on. Then there are his scores on the various aptitude and personality tests he had to take. There's also information on when his application was approved, the date of his enlistment and where he was sent for basic training. It also shows that he applied and enlisted with another Kansas City, Missouri, boy. A kid named Alan Meyers. We see that fairly often, where someone enlists with a friend or even a group of friends."

"Hey, Joe," said Ginny. "Alan Meyers is one of the names of his friends that his wife gave us."

"Great. He's just moved up to next on our to-visit list. Corporal, is there anything in the file about where he was stationed or what his assignments were after basic training?" asked Joe.

"No, I'm sorry," answered Corporal Ford. "We only have his enlisting-related information here. For anything after his assignment to basic, you'll need to contact the base he was stationed at."

"Well, thank you very much for your help," concluded Joe.

"My pleasure, sir. Have a great day, everyone."

"You, too," said all three police officers almost simultaneously as they headed for the door.

Chapter 7

About 45 minutes later, they pulled up in front of a three-story row of apartments, one of which was the home of Alan Meyers. After ringing the bell and knocking on the door of apartment 129, it was obvious that no one was home. Checking with the neighbor next door, they learned that Meyers probably was away as the neighbor hadn't seen nor heard him in several weeks. No, he had no idea where Meyers had gone nor when he would be back. "Why don't you check with his mother? She probably knows."

"Uh, great idea. Do you know how we can reach her?" asked Joe.

"Sure. She lives in the next building over. Unit 116."

"Oh. Thanks. We'll head over there now," said Joe.

This time the doorbell was answered almost immediately. But it was by the building superintendent, not Mrs. Meyers.

"Yes, can I help you?"

"Yes, we're looking for Mrs. Meyers. Is she in? I'm Officer Jakowski with the KC police."

"Uh, no. She's not here. She works at the local Piggly Wiggly supermarket, usually from 4 in the afternoon until 11 at night. I'm Ken Sharpe, the building super. Mrs. Meyers has a leak in her kitchen faucet and I agreed that I'd come over and fix it while she's at work today. Is something wrong?"

"Not as far as we know. We just want to ask her a few questions," said Officer Jakowski. "We'll either swing by where she works, or stop back here tomorrow morning. What's the address of the supermarket where she works?"

The superintendent gave them the location, as well as directions how to drive there, and the three officers were quickly back in the car.

"I guess we'll head over to the supermarket," said Officer Jakowski.

"I'd just as soon leave Mrs. Meyers to the morning. I'd like to head over to your station so that we can say hello to Sergeant James before he packs it in for the day. You agree, Ginny?"

"That's a good idea, Joe. I do want to personally thank him for all the help he's provided."

The drive to the police station took longer than normal as they were in the middle of rush hour traffic. During the drive, Ginny called the sergeant to be sure that he was still there and to let him know that they were on their way over. Sergeant James not only agreed to wait for their arrival, he insisted that all four of them get to experience "real Kansas City barbecue" for dinner that evening.

After a few minutes of meet and greet at the station house, followed by a brief discussion of the case, especially the people they had spoken with earlier that day and what they thought they'd learned so far, Sergeant James announced that it was time to have some real barbecue, and at his expense. Joe joined him in his car, while Officer Jakowski and Ginny followed in the patrol car. Fifteen minutes later, both cars were parked in the large lot outside of Danny's Original KC BBQ Pit. As Joe surveyed the old and unkempt shack-like building in front of him, he sure hoped that Sergeant James knew what he was talking about. Looking at the building, Joe, and he was sure Ginny, would not even consider walking inside, much less eating a meal in there, unless the place had been recommended to them by someone whose judgment in these matters they trusted. On the other hand, all of the cars in the parking lot, assuming that this wasn't also a used car dealership, spoke as a pretty good reference.

After a 10-minute or so wait, the four of them were seated at a table near the center of the room. With everyone's approval, Sergeant James ordered for them all, arranging for family-style platters containing just about all the different barbecued items on the menu as well as a good assortment of sides. Everyone ordered local craft beers.

Conversation over dinner was limited, with everyone focused on the food. In between raves about each food tasted, there was a brief discussion of the case.

"So where do you think you are overall?" asked Sergeant James.

"Good question," answered Ginny. "We made a nice step forward when the vic was identified, but things have slowed down since. We're still hoping that the visits we're making out here will help us with the who and the why."

"Hell," said Joe, "We still don't even know for sure if it was murder one or self-defense. All we've got are our suspicions so far."

"Yup, sounds like how many of the cases progress,"

said Sergeant James. "I'm sure things will come together sooner or later as you keep working the leads."

"Yeah, we're sure they will. Just hope it's sooner rather than later," said Ginny.

"Amen to that," added Joe.

Walking out of the restaurant a little more than an hour later, placing one hand on her stomach, Ginny said "Thanks again for dinner. That was delicious. I'm stuffed to the point that I don't think I'll want to eat for a week."

"You're most welcome," said Sergeant James. "We always eat a lot when we come here. But this time, with you first timers, we had to order more than usual so you could get to taste everything. Kansas City barbecue is world renowned for good reason."

"It sure is," agreed Joe. "Everything was delicious, but those burnt ends were at the top of the list."

"Yeah. They're a true specialty of Kansas City. Well, it's time to get you two off to your hotel. You don't want to lose out on any of your beauty sleep. Again, thanks for visiting us. And we're glad to be able to help. Officer Jakowski will get you over to your hotel and then pick you up in the morning. He's yours for tomorrow until he has you back at the airport. It was a pleasure meeting you both. Good luck on solving this case. Maybe I'll see you in Ohio one of these days."

"Thanks for everything," said Ginny. "We really appreciate all your help and hospitality. We'd love to welcome you to Ohio someday. We don't have burnt ends, but we'll find a couple of local specialties for you."

And with that, after a short drive, they were at the Clearpoint Inn, where they said goodnight to Jakowski and quickly checked in. They dropped their small carry-on bags in their rooms on the second floor directly across from each other, and met back in the hallway to head to the lounge area of the lobby for a nightcap.

It was still fairly early in the evening, and the bar area was almost empty. In addition to the young bartender and middle-aged waitress, only two corner tables were in use — one by three businessmen unwinding at the end of their work day, and the other by a young couple sitting close together, holding hands and sneaking quick kisses.

Joe and Ginny sat down at a small round table in one of the empty corners. The waitress appeared a few minutes later and took their orders — a local craft beer for Joe and a margarita for Ginny. The drinks arrived a few minutes later.

"Not a fancy place," said Joe, "but pleasant enough. And nice and quiet."

"Yes," agreed Ginny.

"I'm sure this place will get busier later, but I like the way it's almost empty now. We'll probably be fast asleep by the time this place starts jumping."

"I'm sure you're right, Joe. We had an early start this morning and a busy day. I'm sure we'll both enjoy a good night's sleep. Well, 'here's to you' or 'bottoms up' or 'cheers,' whichever suits your fancy."

"'Cheers' works just fine."

Twenty minutes later and well into their second round of drinks, Joe said, "Ginny, let me ask you something. Look at those two other occupied tables. Which one are we more like and which one would you rather we be like?"

"Let me see. Well, except for the fact that there are three business people and they're all male at that table over there, we're more like them, unwinding after a day's work."

"And which would you rather be like?"

"Clearly the couple at the other table. In love, or at least immensely enjoying each other's company."

"I'd answer those questions a bit differently. You're right about the three businessmen, but, on the other hand, we are a man and a woman who, even if possibly not in love with each other, do immensely enjoy each other's company."

"Joe, is that you or the beer talking?"

"No, it's me. And, yeah, the beers may have made it easier for me to say it, but it is what I think."

"Joe, I'm not quite sure I understand what you're saying."

"Me neither, Ginny. I do know that I've cared for you a lot, a whole lot in fact, for quite a while, but. ..."

"But what?"

"Well, we're partners and should act that way. We're also great friends, and I don't want to say or do anything to screw that up. And then there's me."

"What does that last statement mean?"

"I've been reluctant, maybe even afraid, to have any, y'know, romantic relationship since Lori and Adam were killed by that damn drunk driver back in Chicago. First, I was sure it was just my loyalty to them, but I've come to realize that a big part, maybe even most of it, is being afraid to have another relationship which could set me up for so much pain again."

"Jeez, Joe. Do you realize that this is the most you've opened up to me in all the time we've been partners? I'm glad, but I don't know how to respond."

"How about telling me your inner thoughts about this, just like I just did."

"OK. Here goes. Joe, we're best friends. I, also, above all don't want to mess that up. And sensing your reluctance to form any new relationships, I've worked hard to control my feelings toward you and to not say or do anything that might upset or scare you."

"Well, that's over now. Now I'm really scared."

"Joe, don't be. We can go as fast or as slowly, or even not at all, as you're comfortable with."

"Thanks, Ginny. I appreciate that. So, how about we sleep together tonight?"

"Joe!"

"No, wait. That's not what I meant. I mean that we literally sleep together. In the same bed, but with our clothes on. And no funny stuff. I just want to hold you and be next to you. I, and probably you also, need to end this lonely existence."

"OK, Joe, but only on one condition. We only do it as long as both of us want to. Any second thoughts by either of us and it's back to our separate rooms."

"Deal. Let's go."

Joe paid for their drinks, leaving a generous tip, and followed Ginny to her room. As agreed, Joe slept in his underwear and Ginny in her nightgown. After cuddling for a few minutes, Ginny fell asleep in Joe's arms. It took Joe a while longer to fall asleep. He was too excited to fall asleep. He couldn't believe that this was happening, that he was holding Ginny in his arms — in bed! He felt happy but petrified at the same time. Yes, Ginny was great as a partner, as a real friend, and now — now as a girlfriend, a lover? It was happening, but he could hardly believe they were together like this. He was glad that they'd finally got their feelings out in the open. That part was good, and not so difficult after all. But now he felt like a ninth-grader again, on his first date with Maryanne Dawson. He caught himself wishing he could get womanly advice from Lori, then realized the absurdity of that. If Lori were still in his life, he'd not be lying here next to Ginny right now.

Joe finally fell asleep. They were both asleep when the alarm clock went off at 7:15. Once up, they said little other than "Good morning," and sheepishly looked at each other as Joe got dressed and headed to his room. Both of them quickly showered and dressed, packed their few belongings and checked out of the hotel. They met in the hotel coffee shop at about 7:45 for breakfast.

"Joe, I really enjoyed last night. It was special."

"Yeah, me, too."

Other than that, their special night was not mentioned by either of them. The awkwardness ended about 45 minutes later when Officer Jakowski arrived to pick them up.

Chapter 8

I t was a little before nine when the three of them pulled up in front of Mrs. Meyers' apartment house and walked to her front door.

"Yes, can I help you?" inquired a gray-haired, 60ish -year old woman wearing a stained housecoat and light brown, furry slippers. Her hair was pinned up and she wore no makeup. "Please excuse my appearance, but Friday is my heavy housecleaning day."

"Not a problem. We're Detectives McFarland and Harris from Jasper Creek, Ohio, and this is Officer Jakowski from the Kansas City PD," said Ginny.

"Oh, my god! Oh, my god! What's wrong? Is it Alan? Did something happen?"

"No, Mrs. Meyers, we're not aware of anything having happened to your son. Sorry if we frightened you. We're looking for some information about one of his friends. We tried your son's apartment, but no one answered. A neighbor thought he was away and suggested you might know where he is," said Joe.

"Whew, what a relief! You scared me half to death."

"We apologize, Mrs. Meyers," said Ginny. "Is Alan away? Do you know where he went and when he'll be back?"

"It sure is a shame that you came all the way out here," said Mrs. Meyers.

"Why do you say that?" asked Ginny.

"Cuz he's back east. In Ohio. Isn't that where you said you're from?"

"Yes, it is," answered Ginny. "Do you know where in Ohio he is? And when he went there? And do you know why?"

"Well, I don't remember where in Ohio. I'm sure he told me, but I'll be darned if I can remember."

"When did he go there? And why?" followed up Joe.

"Well, let me think. He and Paul left here about two months ago. They went to meet with one of their officers from when they were in the Army to see about a job."

"Did you say 'Paul'?" asked Joe.

"Yes, Paul Dalton. Him and Alan been best friends since grade school. They even went and joined the Army at the same time and they were in the Army together for several years."

"May we come in, please, Mrs. Meyers? It's Paul Dalton that we're looking for information about," said Joe.

"Well, sure, come on in. Excuse the mess, but, like I said, I'm in the middle of cleaning."

"We understand. And thank you," replied Ginny.

Mrs. Dalton led them into the small living room, and everyone found their way to a seat.

"Is anything wrong? Did something happen to Paul? I can't believe it's anything bad. Alan didn't say nuthin. I'm sure he woulda called me if there was a problem."

"When did you last hear from your son?" asked Ginny.

"Oh, it was probably a month or so ago. He's a good boy, a real good boy, but you know how youngsters are today. Very independent. And we got into the habit of not being in touch very often when he was in the Army. What with him living far away and often being on missions that he couldn't talk about, not even with me."

"We understand, Mrs. Meyers," said Ginny. "Do you know exactly why he and Paul Dalton went to Ohio?"

"Well, of course I do. I am his mother, you know."

"Yes," said Ginny. "What can you tell us about it?"

"Well, Alan never said so directly, but I'm pretty sure the whole thing was Paul's idea. He was always the one coming up with ideas, and Alan was always the one that tagged along. Paul had found out about this job thing that he and Alan got all excited about."

"What was the job?" asked Ginny.

"It was one of those contractor things for the military. They would have to go to Afghanistan and face the same kind of dangers they faced when they were in the Army. I was dead set against it. But, I'm only his mother."

"Do you recall any of the specifics?" asked Ginny.

"Well, Paul said it wouldn't be that dangerous. They wouldn't really be fighting. They'd just be in the background providing security for some of our military bases, and for big-shot politicians and military brass who visit over there. They would also sometimes help train the Afghan soldiers. Like I said, I was dead set against it, but Alan said it would only be for two or three years and that the pay'd be three or four times what the Army had paid him. And then he joked about being sure that the food would also be a lot better."

"Do you remember the name of the company, or the person they were going to meet in Ohio?" asked Joe.

"Let me think for a minute. My memory ain't as good like it used to be."

"Sure, take your time, Mrs. Meyers."

"The name, I think, was something like Angle Corporation."

"Angle Corporation. Are you sure?" asked Joe.

"It may not be exactly that, but it sure was something like that."

"OK. Thanks. That's helpful. Do you recall the name of the person they were going to meet?"

"No. In fact, I don't think I ever knew his name."

"Do you recall anything about him?" coaxed Joe.

"Not really. Just that he used to be one of the Army big shots when Alan and Paul were in Special Ops. He wasn't the officer right over them. He was somewhere further up the chain, if you know what I mean."

"Yes, we do. And thank you for all your help. Here are cards from Detective Harris and me. Please call one of us if you think of anything else. Also, if you do speak with your son, please have him call one of us."

"I sure will. Paul's a good friend of Alan's and I'm sure Alan'd want to do whatever he can to help. Me too. I do hope that nothing bad has happened to Paul."

"Yes, ma'am. Thank you again for all your help," said Ginny.

And two minutes later, the three of them were back in the patrol car. They spent the next hour with Ginny calling the remaining names that Kristi Dalton had provided. Of the two other couples living in the Kansas City area, she spoke with one of the wives and left a voicemail message for the other couple. She also spoke with one of Paul's buddies still living at Fort Bragg, but she had no phone numbers for the two other friends, one living in Kansas

City and one in Texas. She tried information for both of these, but was unable to get either's phone number. She gained no useful information from the two calls in which she'd made contact.

It was then back to a different Burger King, but the identical lunch to that of the previous day. After that, it was a direct shot to the airport in time for friendly thanks and good-byes with Officer Jakowski, getting their boarding passes, inching through the TSA security line, and arriving at the gate for their 2 p.m. flight back home.

Chapter 9

Joe and Ginny were back at their desks early that next Monday morning. As soon as the chief arrived, they marched into his office.

"Good morning, Chief. Joe and I want to bring you up to date about our Kansas City trip."

"Super. I'd love to hear all about your vacation. Do you also have photos to show me? Or perhaps you brought back some of that Kansas City BBQ for me?"

"Sorry, none of that, Chief. But we did get a couple of nice breaks in the case."

"Oh, how nice. That's like icing on the cake, or would you prefer me to say 'sauce on the brisket?' "

"Ha, ha," said Joe. "But seriously, we think we found out why Paul Dalton, our vic, was in Ohio. And we got the name of a friend who supposedly came here with him from Kansas City."

"Well, that does sound like a step or two of progress. Maybe we'll actually be able to justify the cost of your trip to the taxpayers of this fine city."

"It seems like the two of them came to Ohio for possible jobs. Turns out that one of the former Special Ops officers runs a mercenary firm headquartered here in Ohio. These two guys came east to try to get hired. They'd be sent to Afghanistan for a few years, make good money, especially compared to what they made in the military. They'd be providing military contractor-type work, mostly security and training."

"Have you located the vic's friend yet? Or talked with the mercenary firm?"

"Not yet, Chief. We just got in a little while ago. Those are the two things right at the top of our to-do list," said Ginny.

"Good. It does sound like you two have a couple of solid leads to follow up on. Glad to hear it. And good work."

"Thanks, Chief," said Ginny, as she and Joe left the chief's office, refilled their coffee cups and returned to their desks.

"Wow! It's not often the chief says 'Good work.' We must have done a fantastic job. In fact, Ginny, don't you think that we should take this whole week off to celebrate?"

"Joe, what am I going to do with you? Seriously, let's get cracking on those leads. How about you try to track down the mercenary firm and the ex-officer running it, while I try to locate Alan Meyers?"

"Always so practical and organized. What would I do without you? Let's get to it."

Ten minutes later, Joe raised his head from his computer monitor and said, "OK, I'm all set. How about you?"

"What? How'd you get done so quickly? I'm still just getting started."

"Well, when you're a super cop, these things just come naturally."

"Seriously, Joe. Do you already have the name and address of the mercenary firm? How'd you find it so fast?"

"Actually, it was pretty simple. I went to the Ohio Secretary of State web site. That's where people wanting to start a business in Ohio go to incorporate and select a company name. And one of the first things that pops up is a file that you can search online with the names of all the companies registered to do business in Ohio and the type of business each of the firms is in. They have that for people to check so they don't select a name for their business if that name is already in use in the state."

"Pretty smart."

"I'm not sure if you mean me or the computer system, so I'll assume both. Anyway, I first tried searching for the name that Mrs. Meyers gave us. 'Angle Corporation.' No success. So I kept trying similar names. I finally got a hit with 'Aegis' and found 'Aegis Control Corporation.' From there I went to my super-duper detective tool box."

"Whadda ya mean."

I googled 'Aegis Control Corp' which led to their web site, from which you can learn a lot about the company. What they do, where they're headquartered and who their officers are."

"Come on, Joe, you're killing me with the suspense. What did you learn?"

"Well, they're exactly like all those mercenary firms you read about in the newspaper and see on TV. They operate just about every place the U.S. has troops. They don't do actual fighting, unless, of course, they're attacked. They provide armed guards and security for many of our overseas bases and for high-level officers and politicians who visit. They search people and cars wanting to enter the bases and they protect supply convoys delivering everything — food, equipment and ammo to our troops. In some locations, they also train the locals. Almost all of their employees are ex-military, and most of them are former Seals, Rangers, Delta Force and so on."

"Sounds like these guys don't fool around. Did you get a local address?"

"Sure did. Their headquarters is on East Elm in Columbus. Turns out the company was started a few years ago by a Todd Burke. He was a colonel in the Army and he was the officer in charge of the Special Ops group that I assume Dalton's team was part of. And the company's headquartered here in Ohio because it turns out, again with thanks to Google, ex-Colonel Burke grew up in the suburbs of Columbus."

"Good work. I haven't yet found anything to help us locate Alan Meyers."

"Why don't you put that on hold for now, Ginny? I think we should go pay the ex-colonel a visit."

"OK. Let's go."

Chapter 10

Two hours later, Joe and Ginny were riding up the elevator to the sixth floor of 142 East Elm Street in downtown Columbus. Entering Suite 600, Ginny was surprised. This looked more like the waiting room of a doctor's office than the headquarters of a big, bad mercenary firm. There were several inexpensive, black, fake-leather chairs and a low, wood coffee table. On the table were several magazines. Unlike in the typical doctor's office, however, these all dealt with the military, fighting and weapons. And the walls were covered with photos of tanks and Humvees and employees posing with friends and rifles.

Walking up to the pretty, blond receptionist, Joe quickly waved his badge in front of her. Although he wasn't about to lie, there was no need to volunteer that they were out-of-town rather than Columbus police officers. "Good morning. I'm Detective McFarland and this is Detective Harris. We'd like to see Colonel Burke."

"Oh, I'm sorry, but the colonel isn't in."

"When do you expect him? Shortly?" asked Joe.

"Well, I really don't know. But it won't be shortly. He's out of town and I never know where he's gone or for how long."

"Well, who's in charge when he's away? We'd like to speak with him."

"One moment. I'll check if Captain Watkins is in."

"Thank you," said Joe.

Five minutes later, after receiving a brief phone call, the receptionist led Joe and Ginny through the door behind her desk and down the hall to the end office on the right. The door was open and the receptionist motioned Joe and Ginny to walk in. A tall, dark-haired, attractive woman got up from her desk and shook hands with both detectives.

"Good morning, detectives. I'm Nicole Watkins. Perhaps I can help you since Colonel Burke is not available. Please sit down."

Joe and Ginny introduced themselves and took seats on the couch against the side wall. Watkins sat in the chair facing the couch. After being offered and declining coffee or water, Joe got right into the purpose of their visit, "Ms., or is it Captain, Watkins? Are you second in command under Colonel Burke?"

"Ms. Burke, or Nicole, is fine. I was a captain in the Army, but that was several years ago. I'm second in command here at headquarters. I deal mostly with all of the administrative stuff. Quotes, contracts, finances, employees and all the bureaucratic paperwork that one has to deal with in our type of business. The colonel has several field officers reporting directly to him. I don't really have any say over them or what they do, except if it's administratively related. So, I'm sort of more the office manager than second in command. But perhaps I can still help you."

"Yes, we hope so," said Ginny. "We're trying to track down two men who came here from Kansas City, supposedly to meet with Colonel Burke to discuss being employed by your firm. They were both in Special Ops before."

"Well, they sound like the type of candidates we'd be interested in. Most of our employees come from Special Forces. What are their names? If they've been here or been hired by us, or even just talked with us, we'll have their files in the computer."

"Great," said Ginny. "Their names are Paul Dalton and Alan Meyers, and they're both from Kansas City, Missouri. They would have been here sometime in the past month or two."

"OK. Just give me a few minutes and I'll check our database. Is 'Meyers' 'M-E-Y' or 'M-Y'?"

"It's 'M-E-Y-E-R-S,' " responded Ginny.

"OK, I should have the files in a minute."

And a few minutes later, "OK, got them. Both are in the database."

"That's great," said Joe. What can you tell us?"

"Well, let's see. I've got Dalton's info first. It seems that he and the other fellow, Alan Meyers, had an initial meeting with Colonel Burke July 2nd. Colonel Burke usually structures the process that way. He'll first schedule just an information sharing session where he gives some information about our company and what it would be like to work for us. He tries to give an objective view of the good and the bad, including the risks, the periods of boredom, the time away from home, the weather where they're likely to be assigned and so on. He tells the potential recruit to think about it for a few days and to then call to make an appointment if he wants to apply and start the rigorous evaluation process. Looks like he held the bulk of this first session with both of the men at the same time."

"What do you mean by 'the bulk'?" asked Ginny.

"Whenever Colonel Burke meets with two or more potential recruits at the first meeting, he always then spends at least a few minutes at the end of the session with each one individually."

"Why? What's the reason for that?" asked Joe.

"He's found that sometimes someone has something important to say or ask, but they're reluctant to do so in front of others. And in some cases, their military career contained confidential aspects that they couldn't say in front of others. Colonel Burke has retained his security clearances, so they could tell him things when others weren't present."

"At that first meeting, did you gather any detailed information about the two potential candidates?" asked Joe.

"Not really. They probably discussed their military careers in very general terms, talked about when and why they left the service, what they've been doing since then and why they might want to join Aegis."

"If some of that detail is in the file, we'd love to get a copy," said Ginny.

"I can't give you a copy to keep, but before you leave, I can arrange for you two to go to one of our spare offices and review the files online."

"That would be helpful," responded Ginny.

"What happened after that first meeting?" asked Joe.

"Hmm. Let's see. Oh here it is. It looks like Mr. Meyers called back two days later and scheduled for himself and for Mr. Dalton to come back in for almost a full day of tests. Intelligence, emotional stability, personality and so on. These are a complete battery of computerized tests. These took place for both of them on July 8th. At the end of the tests, they then both scheduled July 12th for a series of one-on-one interviews with some of our executives, a couple of field operators and an industrial psychologist."

"That sounds pretty extensive," said Ginny.

"You're right. Both the testing and the interviews are very thorough. We really try to weed out all but the best before we proceed to a second interview with Colonel Burke, after which a hiring decision is made."

"Can you tell us the results of the tests and interviews?" asked Joe.

"No. I'm sorry. That's confidential. Like medical records. Unless you have a warrant, Colonel Burke is the only one who could make a policy exception and share that information with you."

"We understand. So what happened next?" asked Joe.

"We called them a couple of days later and scheduled their second interviews with the colonel for July 19th, one at 9:00 a.m. and the other at 11:00.

"Early on the 19th, Mr. Meyers called. During that call, and again when he came in later that morning, he said that Mr. Dalton was very interested in proceeding but that a family emergency came up that would require him to be out of town for a week or two, and that he would call to reschedule his follow-up meeting as soon as he got back."

"Did Meyers say what Dalton's emergency was?" asked Joe.

"No. Just that it was a family emergency requiring him to leave town."

"OK. So what took place next with Meyers?" asked Joe.

"Turned out that he was very interested in the job and, based upon all the written and physical tests, as well as the interviews, we were interested in hiring him."

"And?" prodded Joe.

"We hired him."

"Good for him," said Joe. "We'd like to talk with him."

"Well, that won't be too easy."

"Now, look, Ms. Watkins. We're investigating a serious crime and your stonewalling us is not going to be very well appreciated by a lot of people who matter a lot!" barked Joe.

"Please. Please. Let me explain. I'm not trying to be difficult. It's just that Mr. Meyers is already on assignment."

"That was quick," said Ginny.

"Yes, it was, but that happens fairly often with us. His military training and experience was just what we needed, he had no job that he had to give quitting notice to and he was already here. With no ties other than a hotel room. Not even a wife with whom he had to discuss his decision."

"Where is he?" continued Joe.

"I don't know exactly where at the moment. But his assignment base is Bagram Airfield, about 25 miles northeast of Kabul, Afghanistan."

"Oh, I see," said Joe sheepishly.

"We'd have to check whether he's currently at the airfield or out in the field. In fact, I can check that while you're looking through the two computerized files. If he's on the airfield, or when he returns, we can set up an Internet link where you and he can see and speak with each other."

"Thank you. We'd appreciate that. One other thing," said Joe. "Has Paul Dalton gotten back yet and have you hired him?"

"Hold on. Let me check the computer file. Here it is. No, we haven't heard anything from him since Mr. Meyers informed us that Mr. Dalton had that family emergency to deal with. I have no idea whether he's still away or if he decided this job wasn't for him."

"OK. Thanks. Why don't you set us up to view their two files now, while you find out when we can have that Internet call with Alan Meyers," said Joe.

"Will do. Follow me, please."

Joe and Ginny found themselves in a cramped, windowless office, not much bigger than a broom closet. Watkins had them sit in front of the computer monitor on the desk after she pulled up the files for Paul Dalton and Alan Meyers. "Feel free to take as many notes as you want. I'll be back as soon as I know something about Mr. Meyers' whereabouts and availability."

Joe and Ginny spent the next 15 minutes going through the two files and taking some notes, but they didn't really see anything they thought would help their investigation. Watkins came back in and said that Mr. Meyers was in the middle of a three-day security assignment in Kabul and that he should be back at the base sometime the day after tomorrow. After explaining that Afghanistan was nine hours ahead of Ohio, Watkins scheduled the phone call for Wednesday at 8 a.m. Ohio time. Joe and Ginny thanked her, said they'd be back on Wednesday for the call and headed for the door and their drive back to Jasper Creek.

Joe spent the next day and a half working on a few other cases and also trying, with no success, to get a handle on what Dalton might have been up to and where he'd been from the time of his initial meetings at Aegis until his death. Joe was doing this alone as Ginny was home with a wicked stomach flu — nausea, diarrhea, fever, chills and weakness. Joe called her a couple of times during the day to see how she was doing, but he didn't want to call too often. He felt that Ginny needed her rest. He did decide, however, to visit her after work.

It took longer than usual after he rang the bell, but Ginny, wearing an old robe over her nightgown, her hair uncombed and her face devoid of makeup, eventually got to the door and opened it. "Joe, what are you doing here? I look like hell."

"Joe? You mean Dr. McFarland. I'm here to take care of my favorite patient. And, believe me, even on your sickest day, you look a whole lot better than hell. In fact, you look pretty darn good." And with that, from behind his back, he held out a small bouquet of red roses and two cans of chicken noodle soup.

"Oh, Joe, you're so sweet. Come in."

A few minutes later, Ginny was sitting in the kitchen with a blanket wrapped around her, and Joe was carrying two bowls of hot soup from the stove to the table. "Here, Ginny, this is the best known medicine for what ails you."

"Joe, as well as I know you, you do still manage to amaze me once in a while. But, seriously, thank you so much."

"Don't mention it. This is what partners and best friends are for. Plus, I want you to get better quickly. I'm tired of having to do all the work myself."

"Don't worry. I called the doctor. Apparently there's a 24-hour bug going around. I should be good as new in a day or so."

"Glad to hear it. Actually, I got really worried and scared."

"Why, Joe?"

"I'm not sure. I know it's totally irrational. But my brain started going wild, comparing this to how I lost Lori 'cause of that dumb drunk driver."

"Oh, Joe. I'm sorry."

"You've got nothing to apologize for, Ginny. And please don't think I'm confusing or comparing you and Lori. I'm not."

"I never thought you were, Joe."

"I never really described in full detail how badly I fell apart after the accident. I went around wishing it had been me instead of them, or at least that I was with them in the car. I really didn't want to live. I've gotten a lot better over the years, but I'm still not totally over it. I'm not sure I ever will be."

"Oh, Joe, I'm so sorry. You need to keep recovering, but there's no reason to expect you'll ever get fully over it or forget what happened. You have to get back to fully living your life despite it. What can I do to help you?"

Joe turned away from Ginny and quickly ran his hand across his face, wiping the tears that had formed and started to roll down his cheeks. "Nothing, Ginny. There's nothing for you to do. Just being yourself and showing how you care means the world to me. Just ignore this little childish outburst."

"Joe, it's not little. And it's not childish. In fact, not that I like you to be sad, but your crying in front of me means a lot to me. You're my best friend. And you can do or say anything in front of me. And I will do anything I can to help you. Always."

"Ginny, thanks. But sorry for the outburst in any event. And now it's time to help my best friend get back into bed and get a good night's sleep."

Five minutes later, Ginny was fast asleep. Joe made sure she was covered well, washed the soup bowls and spoons, and quietly left the apartment. Driving home, he couldn't stop thinking about how much he cared about Ginny, as a partner, a best friend, and more.

Chapter 11

As predicted, Ginny made a speedy recovery. She and Joe were on the road bright and early Wednesday morning as they knew they'd be fighting rush-hour traffic. They arrived at Aegis a few minutes before 7:45, in plenty of time to say hello to Watkins, get cups of freshly brewed coffee and be seated back in the small office in front of the monitor before 8 a.m.

"I think we should get jobs here," said Joe.

"Why? What are you talking about? If all the offices are this size, I'd be claustrophobic in no time."

"Yeah, you're right about the office. But, boy, this coffee is a big step up from the Jasper Creek PD premium blend."

"I agree with you on the coffee, Joe. But I'm not sure I'm ready to switch careers for it."

"And all this time I thought you were good at setting the right priorities," chuckled Joe.

A few minutes before eight, Watkins and a technician from the IT Department came in. The technician patched the call into a similar little room at the air base in Afghanistan. Both Watkins and the technician left the room, giving Joe and Ginny a phone extension to call if there were any technical problems once the call started and to call when their phone call was finished. The technician at Bagram Airfield gave similar instructions to Meyers before he walked out.

"Hello. Hello. Can you hear me?" asked Meyers.

"Yes, we can. We can also see you on our monitor. Mr. Meyers, I'm Detective McFarland and this is Detective Harris. We're calling you from the Aegis Control offices in Columbus, Ohio."

"Is everything all right? Is it my mom? What happened?"

"Everything is fine with your mother. At least it was a few days ago when we saw her. She would like you to call her more often, though," said Ginny.

"Yeah, that sounds like her. Then why are you calling?"

"Do you know where Paul Dalton is, Mr. Meyers?" asked Joe.

"Uh, no. Did something happen to Paul? Is he OK?"

"When did you last see or speak to him?" asked Ginny.

"Uh, it was about two weeks ago. When I left to have my second meeting with Colonel Burke at Aegis."

"Where did Mr. Dalton go?" asked Joe.

"Damned if I know. It was the weirdest thing."

"What was?"

"Well, we had gone out and done a bit of heavy drinking the night before. To celebrate what we were sure was going to be great job offers."

"Where was this?" asked Joe.

"Downtown Columbus. Don't ask me where. We roamed from bar to bar and pretty soon neither of us could see straight."

"OK, and then what?" asked Joe.

"Early the next morning, back in our hotel room, with a bit of a hangover, we talked about the jobs we were sure we were going to get with Aegis. We were both really pumped up about the jobs. The excitement and the money."

"Then what happened?" asked Ginny.

"While we were just gabbing about what to expect when we met with Colonel Burke later that morning, out of the blue, Paul said he had to hold off for a bit. I assumed he meant hold up our discussion for two minutes while he went to take a leak. But no. He said that something had come up and he had to head out of town for a couple of weeks. He said I should proceed on my own with Aegis and that he'd catch up to me in a couple of weeks."

"Did he say what came up?"

"No. And that's what's so weird. I asked him a few times, but he wouldn't say anything. He just said it had to do with family. He and I have been tight buds for years. We told each other everything, and I mean everything, until this time."

"Do you have any idea what it could have been?" asked Joe.

"No friggin' idea at all. And I checked with Captain Watkins a few days ago, and Paul still hadn't called in to reschedule his next appointment. What's going on? Is Paul in trouble? Did something happen to him?"

"Mr. Meyers, where did you and Paul stay while you were in Columbus?"

"We found a zero star, or maybe it was a minus-two star, motel near the center of town. They didn't even take credit cards. We had to pay cash for the room. The name was something like the Little Budget Inn."

"Do you remember the address?" asked Joe.

"It was on West Broad Street, but I don't remember the number."

"That's OK. How'd you two get from Kansas City to Ohio?" asked Ginny.

"We took the bus. I left my car for my mom. If I got this job, which I did, I knew I wouldn't be needing my car for two or three years. And Paul sold his car before we left Kansas City. He was pretty sure we'd both get the jobs and he said he'd just buy a different car if he didn't get the job.

"When we got to Ohio, I rented the cheapest pile of junk that Rent-A-Wreck had."

"Mr. Meyers, any idea why Mr. Dalton would have gone to Jasper Creek here in Ohio?"

"Where? I never even heard of that place. I sure don't know why Paul woulda gone there. Did something happen to him there?"

Seeing a slight nod from Joe, Ginny responded. "Yes, I'm afraid it did. We're sorry to have to tell you that Mr. Dalton was killed there a few nights ago. Shot."

"Oh, my god! No! I can't believe it! Why Paul? We were just together a little while ago. Was it a robbery?"

"We don't think so, but our investigation is still in its early stages," answered Ginny.

"Have you told his wife yet?"

"Yes, we have."

"I know they were having some troubles. Paul somehow got freaked out before he left Special Ops, and he became real tough to live with. And them with a little kid. Poor Kristi, I really feel for her. Jeez!"

"Do you know what happened to him in Special Ops?" asked Joe.

"Not specifically. All the shit we saw and the crap we had to do and had to put up with messed up most of us. But it seemed to hit Paul harder than most."

"Were you in the same unit as Paul?"

"Well, we were in the same location. But we were on two different teams. We saw each other a lot on the base, but our teams only did a few joint missions together."

"Do you know exactly what got him so spooked?"

"No. I actually didn't even notice any change in Paul until we were back home in Kansas City for a while. I don't know if he hadn't changed earlier or if I just didn't see it sooner. In any event, since all of our missions were classified, I couldn't give you any of the details even if I knew them."

"Understood," said Joe. "Well, that's about it from our end. At least for now. We may come back at some point if we have more questions. And if you think of or learn anything else, please let Ms. Watkins know and she'll arrange another call."

"OK."

"Thank you. And again, we're very sorry for your loss."

"Yeah, thanks. Just get the bastard or bastards who killed him."

And with that, the screen went blank. Ginny called the extension that Watkins had given them, and the technician was immediately back in the room to shut down the system. A quick good-bye with Watkins, and Joe and Ginny were back in the car.

"Joe, before we head back home, let's see if we can find that motel and swing by there."

"Ginny, are you actually propositioning me?"

"No, smart ass. I'm trying to show you how good detective work is done. This is a new lead that we should follow up."

"Good idea. Why don't you see if you can find it on your smartphone?"

"OK. Gimme a couple of minutes," agreed Ginny. And then a few minutes later, "I got it, Joe. Meyers wasn't far off. It's Little Buddha Inn, not Little Budget Inn. It's at 788 West Broad."

"Well done. I'm heading there now."

A quick look at the outside of the rundown motel, which fit nicely with the rundown neighborhood, told both detectives not to be too optimistic about gaining much useful information. A brief discussion with the manager in the front office confirmed that the two men had rented there for a while, but had since checked out. The manager couldn't remember exactly when or which room they had rented, and since the motel only accepted cash and did not have any type of reservation system or registration log, the interview ended rather quickly.

Back on the highway toward Jasper Creek, Ginny stated the obvious. "Well, that sure was a big help. What a dump!"

"The good news, Ginny, is that he didn't remember what room they were in."

"Why's that good news?"

"Because if he had remembered, being the loyal and

dedicated detectives that we are, we'd have felt obligated to search the room."

"And?"

"My guess is that the bedbugs in those rooms are large enough for each of us to have easily lost at least an arm."

"Jeez, that's gross. Thanks. I'll probably never get that image out of my head now."

"Just callin' 'em like I see 'em," replied Joe.

"To change the subject, Joe, that video phone call was pretty snazzy. Even though the picture wasn't perfectly clear and it sometimes jumped a bit or froze for a few seconds, it was a lot more useful than a plain phone call. You feel more connected to the person you were talking to."

"Yeah. And it also lets you read their body language, which you sure can't do on a regular phone call."

"Very true."

"Hey, Ginny, why don't we recommend that the chief get us a system like that?"

"Sure, Joe, go for it if you feel like wasting your breath. Why don't you also suggest a helicopter for the department? We're lucky that the chief authorizes a few new pens and notepads once in a while. Anyhow, that video system only works if the person you're talking to has the same, or at least a similar, system."

"Good point, Ginny. We're probably a bit premature. But I bet a system like that will be commonplace sometime in the future."

"Yeah, I'm sure you're right. Once again you've proven yourself to be a man ahead of his time."

"Oh, gimme a break."

"But seriously, I do think we had a good discussion with Meyers. Although he didn't know what happened to the vic, he was able to fill us in why they came to Ohio and when Dalton split from him. And why Dalton split, or at least the reason he gave Meyers."

"Agreed. And he did seem genuinely surprised when we told him Dalton had been killed."

"Yes, he did. We need to focus in on why the vic cancelled his second interview at the last minute."

"Yeah, especially since he seemed to keep the details of his reason a big secret from his best bud."

"Very true."

"Hey, Joe, how about a small lecture while we're driving back to Jasper Creek. I'm confused about Special Operations versus Special Forces and all that stuff. The only group I think I'm somewhat clear about is the Navy SEALs."

"OK, I'll try. But the organization and the names are a bit confusing. Not sure if the military does that on purpose or if it's typical government bureaucracy. Probably some of each."

"OK, go for it. I'm ready to get educated. Actually, were you in Special Operations when you served?"

"I can tell you that, Ginny, but then I'd have to kill you. But seriously, no, I wasn't. I was just in the plain old Army infantry. All guts and no glory as we used to say. Well, here goes my mini-lecture.

" 'Special operations' is just a general term that refers to specialized, elite forces. And it's not only the U.S. that has these. Many countries have their special operations forces. You may have heard of Pakistan's Special Service Group, Israel's Sayeret Matkal, Russia's Spettsnaz or England's Special Air Services."

"Yes, I've heard of a few of those. But what about the U.S. specifically?"

"Jeez, stop rushing the professor. In the U.S., every branch of the military, even the Coast Guard, has one or more special operations groups. Even the CIA has one. These just refer to some elite part of their organization that often gets the tricky or secret assignments. The Navy SEALS, as you said earlier, are probably the most well-known. They've been on several high-profile assignments. The SEALs, in general, love publicity. And within the SEALs, Team 6 is the crème de la crème.

"The Army has several special operations groups. There are the Green Berets, named for the caps they wear. Their official name is Army Special Forces. Then there are the Army Rangers, which is an elite light infantry group. Then, made up almost exclusively of applicants from the Rangers and Green Berets, is the elite of the elite within the Army, called Delta Force. This group is probably roughly equivalent to the Navy SEALs. The difference is that while the SEALs seek publicity, Delta Force seeks secrecy and privacy. In fact, the military has never even confirmed the existence of Delta Force."

"Wow. Pretty amazing. Were Dalton and Meyers in Delta Force?"

"We don't know, and the military won't say. But I doubt it. It's a very small number of soldiers who make it into

Delta. Plus these two seem too young and not in the military long enough to have made it."

"OK, Joe. Thanks for the lecture."

"My pleasure."

A quick stop, gas for the car plus burgers and fries for the two detectives, and they were back at their desks by 12:30.

Chapter 12

"See, I told you."

"What are you talking about?" asked Ginny.

"This coffee stinks compared to what we had at Aegis."

"Can't argue with that. Hey, Joe. This looks like the yearbook the dean at Dalton's college agreed to send us," said Ginny as she picked up a large envelope from her desk and began opening it. "Sure is a nice change when someone actually does what he says he will."

"You can say that again."

Ginny took the next 15 minutes to carefully go through the yearbook, writing down all the numbers of the pages containing references to or pictures of Dalton or Meyers.

"Nothing here jumps out at me," said Ginny as she rolled her chair around the desks and next to Joe's chair so that they could look at the selected pages together.

"I agree. Why don't you Xerox the pages you selected. Just in case. Then we can mail the book back to the dean."

Ginny went and made the photocopies, typed a short thank-you note to the dean, put the yearbook and note into a new, addressed envelope and dropped it in the out-going-mail bin next to the coffee machine.

"OK, where do we go now based on what we learned from our video call with Meyers?"

"Very pertinent question, Ginny. Probably the very

same question that the chief will be asking us anytime now."

"Let's review what we know so far. We know that Dalton came back changed from his tours overseas. We also know how he and his wife drifted apart and how he left her."

"Right. And we now know why Dalton and Meyers came to Ohio. How they had their initial interviews and tests at Aegis. We also know that Meyers followed up with Aegis and got hired by them."

"Yeah. Also the weird way that Dalton didn't go back for the follow-up interview. But we don't know why for sure."

"Very true," said Joe. "We also have no idea how or why Dalton wound up in Jasper Creek, much less in that abandoned warehouse."

"Right. We also know that he was killed there. It's not just a dump site."

"That about covers it, Ginny. Now what?"

"Besides waiting for the ME's findings, which probably will confirm but not add to what we already know, we need to focus on trying to find out why Dalton didn't continue the interviewing process with Aegis. And also what he was doing in that warehouse."

"Sounds like good ideas. But easier said than done."

"That's why we get paid the big bucks, Joe. I'm going to swing by the medical examiner's office and either get some conclusions or light a fire under him. I'll also stop by to see if there's anything new from the crime scene folks or with fingerprint analysis."

"OK. While you're doing that, I'll go bring the chief up

to date," said Joe as he stood up and headed for the chief's office.

"Hey, Chief. Got a minute? I want to fill you in on the warehouse homicide."

"Come on in and have a seat. An arrest would be much preferable to an update. As you had predicted, I'm getting pressure from the politicos to get this one solved pronto. A murdered war hero isn't the image that the Chamber of Commerce or tourist bureau wants."

"Understood. But we're only lowly detectives, not magicians. So you'll have to settle for an update for now."

"OK. Update away."

Joe spent the next ten minutes bringing the chief up to date — what he and Ginny had done so far, what they knew and what they didn't know and what their next steps were. The chief thanked him, encouraged him and Ginny to try to make progress as fast as they could, and then looked up at the doorway — his not-so-subtle hint that the meeting was over.

Joe returned to his desk. About 20 minutes later, Ginny was sitting back down at her desk across from Joe's.

"Welcome, back. The chief's up to speed. Whatcha learn from your wanderings?"

"Wanderings? High-level detective-follow-up stuff is the technical term for what I was doing."

"Well, I beg your forgiveness, Ms. Super Sleuth."

"OK. You're forgiven. This time. Anyhow, a few interesting tidbits from the ME. He confirmed that one or both of the shots was the cause of death. They were both potentially fatal shots, fired one right after one another, so it's impossible to tell which one was the actual kill shot.

He also slightly narrowed down the TOD estimate, from his initial 12-20 hours to 12-16 hours."

"Let's see. We were with him about 5 that morning, so the time of death would have been between 1 and 5 p.m. the previous day. Right?"

"Yes, that's the range. Daylight the entire time period. The other piece of interesting info is that the victim had a significant amount of propofol in his system."

"Sounds familiar. But what exactly is it?"

"The ME explained that it's a very strong anesthetic, widely used with surgeries. It's given by injection and it'll make you unconscious in a matter of seconds."

"Sounds like I could use a shot of that when I go to bed every night."

"I don't think so, Joe. This is pretty potent stuff. And the ME said it's fast becoming one of the preferred drugs for abuse. People fall unconscious and then wake up feeling euphoric. It's widely available in hospitals and surgery centers, and controls are often sloppy or nonexistent. Apparently, many hospital and clinic workers steal it for their own use or to sell it to others. This is most likely how our killer or whoever injected the drug into Dalton got his or her hands on it."

"Sounds likely. It also raises the possibility that the vic was knocked out someplace else and then brought to the warehouse. From the blood splatter at the scene, we know that he was actually shot at the warehouse, but this might explain why he was there."

"Good point."

"Learn anything else?" asked Joe.

"No, that's it. Also, nothing new from the fingerprints guy. Found several other prints in the warehouse, but none are the vic's or the building owner's. No idea whose they might be, nor how long, possibly even years, they've been there. He's still running them through the Fed's fingerprint database. My guess is that most of them belong to some of the druggies and homeless folks who've used the building. Perhaps even tenants from years ago."

"Well, OK. At least we got a few potentially useful pieces of info from the ME. Now what?"

"I think we've got to focus on why Dalton didn't go back to Aegis with his buddy Meyers. Perhaps we should try again to see Colonel Burke. There might have been more discussion in his private chat with Dalton than what made its way into his file."

"Good idea, Ginny. I'll call Aegis and see if he's back from his trip yet."

Joe called and learned that Burke was still out of town. He asked and was put through to Nicole Watkins. She explained that the colonel was currently in South America. She didn't know exactly where or when he'd be back, but she thought she could probably arrange for Joe and Ginny to speak with him by phone.

"That would be great," said Joe. "We appreciate your help."

"Glad to be of help. Let me try to get in touch with him and see if I can't schedule a time for him to call you. I'll get back to you as soon as I've contacted him."

"Thanks," said Joe, after which he gave Watkins his phone number and hung up.

A few minutes later, Watkins called Joe back and said that the colonel could call him in about two hours. Joe readily agreed.

Chapter 13

Exactly two hours later, Joe's phone rang. It was, indeed, Colonel Burke. Joe answered the call and then transferred it to the conference room where he and Ginny could talk over the speaker phone without all the background noise from the PD bullpen.

"Hello, Colonel. Can you hear me OK?"

"Yes, fine. Good afternoon, detective. Sorry I've been so hard to get hold of these past few days."

"Not a problem, Colonel. We appreciate your calling us. I have you on the speaker. My partner, Detective Harris, is here with me."

"Hello, detective."

"Hello, Colonel."

"Detectives, Nicole told me that you want to speak about Paul Dalton, whom I met with a few weeks ago. I barely recalled him until Nicole summarized his file to me and refreshed my memory. How can I help you?"

"We're trying to trace his comings and goings after his first meeting with you. We understand that you met with him and his friend, Alan Meyers, first both together and then each one individually."

"Yes, that's correct. After some general information and questions with both of them, I spent a few minutes with each of them separately. That allows me to focus on each of them, and it also gives them the opportunity to say or ask things they might not want to if others are present."

"That makes sense," said Ginny. "What, if anything, stood out to you regarding Paul Dalton?"

"Well, I do remember that his friend, Meyers, seemed well balanced and the type of candidate we're looking for. In fact, we later wound up hiring him. Dalton never came back for a second interview."

"Do you know why?" asked Joe.

"No idea. But I'm not surprised."

"Why do you say that, Colonel?" asked Ginny.

"Well, I couldn't be sure based just on a brief meeting with him, but I sensed that he seemed to have some emotional problems from his time overseas. He seemed moody, extremely negative about the military and especially his direct superiors. In fact, he seemed almost depressed. It also seems that he'd had difficulties integrating back into civilian life after he left the service. He couldn't hold down a job, split with his wife, and so on. These types of issues were pretty much confirmed by the tests he took and the interviews he went through in Columbus."

"We appreciate your openness, Colonel," said Joe. "Anything else you can tell us?"

"No, that's about it. Remember, I probably was with him only for 45 minutes or so along with that other fellow, and then perhaps 15 or 20 minutes alone with him."

"OK, well thank you very much, Colonel. If you think of anything else, please let us know."

"I sure will. And you're very welcome. But it might help me if you explained what happened and what it is that you're investigating. Did something happen to Dalton? Or is he just missing? Or did he commit some crime?"

"He was killed. We're trying to find out by who and why?"

"Oh. What a shame. Well, good luck with finding his killer. Good-bye for now."

"Good-bye."

After hanging up, Ginny asked, "Joe, do you think that last 'good luck' comment was sincere? Or was it sarcastic?"

"Good question. I was thinking the same thing, and my answer is "I don't know." "

"One more person to keep on our suspect list for now."

"Yup."

And with that, Joe and Ginny refilled their coffee mugs and returned to their desks.

Chapter 14

A round four o'clock that afternoon, Ginny got a call from the Patrol Division shift commander. After completing the call, Ginny said to Joe, "That was Patrol. As part of their search of the streets around the warehouse, they came across a homeless addict in possession of a nice, fairly new cellphone. He claims he found it in the street, but couldn't remember exactly where. Back at the PD, they determined the phone belongs, or belonged, to Paul Dalton. They say there are several voicemail and text messages that we probably want to go through."

"Hell, yes. We definitely want to. Let's go."

Joe and Ginny went downstairs to the Patrol Division offices. One of the techs sat with them in an office as they listened to the voicemail messages and read the text messages. Most of them were quite old and not of any value. But one voicemail message, received the day before Dalton and Meyers were scheduled to have their second interviews with Burke, was very promising.

"Hello, Mr. Dalton. This is Sergeant Andrews at Aegis Control. Colonel Burke asked me to give you a call. First, he wants to thank you for visiting. He was very impressed with you and your background and looks forward to continuing to work the hiring process with you. Second, and this is a bit sensitive, he'd like to meet with you to discuss something important about the friend you came in with, Alan Meyers. But please do not say anything to Mr. Meyers.

"Early tomorrow morning when you and he are scheduled to return to Aegis, you need to tell Mr. Meyers that something came up and you can't join him. Encourage him to go ahead without you, telling him you'll make it back to Aegis at a later date. Then, once he leaves for Aegis, you should pack your stuff and move out of your hotel. Find some nondescript hotel on the other side of the city, check in using a false name and pay with cash. Then, next Tuesday at 10 in the morning, go to where South Glenwood Avenue passes under the I-70 West Freeway. The colonel will be waiting there to talk with you, both about Mr. Meyers and about your future with Aegis. Thanks. And sorry for all the secrecy, but this is often par for the course here at Aegis. Bye."

"Wow," said Ginny. "This sure opens up a whole bunch of stuff for us. It makes it pretty clear why Dalton didn't return to Aegis and why Meyers couldn't understand why."

"Yeah, and it sure shines a whole different light on our friends at Aegis. So much for the honesty and openness of Burke and Watkins."

"You got that right."

Carefully maintaining a secure chain of evidence, and filling out all the forms, Joe and Ginny arranged for a recorded copy of the voicemail message to be made and the message typed out, and for the cell phone to be carefully logged and stored in the evidence locker. They also spoke with the patrol officer who had found the homeless person with the cell phone and asked him to carefully and thoroughly write up his notes, as they might eventually be needed in court.

Back at their desks, Ginny commented, "Boy, I bet Dalton was really torn. I'm sure he didn't like keeping secrets from his best friend and sneaking around behind his back. On the other hand, he probably felt he had to do what he was asked so that he wouldn't mess up his hiring chances at Aegis."

"Yeah, that Watkins or Burke clearly knew exactly how to play him."

"Yup, like a Stradivarius violin," said Ginny. "What's our next move?"

"We clearly need to revisit our good friends at Aegis. Perhaps we can catch them off guard if they don't know what we know. But, let's first get some background info on both of them. We should know all we can about them before we meet them again."

"Full agreement. I'll get started on that background stuff now," said Ginny. "We also still need to figure out why Dalton went to or was brought to that specific warehouse where he was shot. It's possible that it was just chosen at random, but it's also possible that it was anything but random. And I think we should at some point take a look at that corner in Columbus where Dalton was told to meet with Burke."

"All good points, Ginny."

Ginny spent about an hour beginning their efforts on these next steps. But the day was soon over. They were both happy to leave the piles of papers on their desks and head to their homes for quick dinners and a good night's sleep.

Chapter 15

By eight the next morning, they were both back at their desks. Ginny went to work using all of her normal sources to gather everything she could about Burke and Watkins. Joe used some of his former Army contacts in pursuit of the same type of information.

Soon after lunch, Ginny had pulled together everything that she and Joe had been able to learn. "OK, Joe, I think we got everything we're likely to get for now on our two friends at Aegis. Ready for a quick summary of what we found out?"

"Sure. Go for it."

"OK. Colonel Todd Burke seems to be exactly as advertised. Born in Pittsburgh, but his family moved to Canton when he was a young boy. Went to grade school and high school in Canton and then to the University of Canton. Graduated with a degree in business administration."

"And then?" asked Joe.

"Right after graduation, he joined the Army. After a few years, he transferred into the Army Rangers, where he remained for the rest of his Army career. Over the years, he served in various Latin American countries, Kuwait and Iraq."

"Yeah, I was lucky to get even that amount of detail about his Army career," said Joe. "The Army is very close-lipped about their special forces."

"Glad you've got 'friends in all the right places,' Joe. Want me to sing that song for you?"

"No thanks. I've heard you sing before."

"Boy, you're brutal. You sure know how to hurt a girl. Anyway, continuing on. He retired as a full colonel in 2010, after 30 years of service. Later that same year, he started Aegis Control. Still owns 100% of it, and its revenues are estimated to be about $100 million per year."

"Not too shabby."

"Right. And by the way, about three-quarters of their business is from the U.S. military, the rest is from a few allied militaries and from private companies and individuals wanting various security services."

"Good summary, Ginny. I checked his record. He's had a few speeding tickets, and that's it. Oh yeah, married and divorced twice. No kids."

"That about covers it. Let's switch to his sidekick, Superwoman. Her background's a lot shorter and simpler. Born in '76, she grew up in New York City. Graduated with a degree in biology from Hofstra University on Long Island. Interestingly, she then became a paramedic in one of the New York City suburbs for three years."

"Hmm, interesting indeed. She surely would know all about propofol and how to administer it."

"Exactly my thought. She then became a medic in the Army, and soon transferred to a more administrative role. She left the Army after eight years. In late 2011, she moved to Columbus to join Aegis. Not sure how she and Aegis hooked up. Doesn't look like she and Burke ever crossed paths in the Army. Briefly married while she was a paramedic. Never married again and no kids."

"I hate to pat ourselves on the back, but we did a good job of gathering all this info in short order."

"Joe, we deserve the pat on the back. And if we don't give it to ourselves, no one else will."

"Fair enough. We're on a roll. Let's keep going. Why don't you schedule another meeting with our Super-woman paramedic and, if he's ever in this part of the world, with her boss. I'll try to figure out why that specific warehouse was chosen."

"Sounds good."

A few minutes later, "OK, Joe, we have a meeting with Watkins tomorrow at 10. She has no idea when Burke will be back, but she doubts by tomorrow. And, after we meet with her tomorrow, we can swing by that location where Burke and Dalton presumably met."

"Good. By the way, so far I'm still no place on figuring out what's special about that warehouse. Maybe it was just randomly chosen among the several abandoned ones in that area."

"To quote my illustrious crime-fighting partner: 'Randomness is first cousin to, and only slightly less likely to occur than, coincidence.' "

"I know. I know. I'm just saying."

Nothing significant happened the rest of the afternoon.

Chapter 16

Joe and Ginny were on the highway heading to Columbus the next morning. They left early enough to beat most of the morning traffic. They arrived early, parked the car and had time for Egg McMuffins — one for Ginny and two for Joe — and large coffees. Over breakfast, Joe and Ginny strategized for their meeting with Watkins.

"How do you think we should play it, Ginny?"

"I think we should be pretty upfront and direct. A bit of a confrontation might break her composure a bit."

"I think you're right. Wanna play the bad guy?"

"I'd love to. But in this case, I think it might be more effective coming from you. Her military background and then working for Aegis probably has her used to men calling the shots."

"OK, my pleasure," said Joe. "Hate to take all the fun from you, but I'll happily play the role."

A short walk around the corner and an elevator ride soon had Joe and Ginny back in Aegis' doctor's office-like lobby. They were clearly recognized. The receptionist welcomed them by name and led them to Watkins' office before Joe and Ginny could announce themselves and say why they were there.

"Good morning, detectives," said Watkins as she stood up, walked to the front of her desk and shook hands with

Joe and Ginny. "I didn't expect to see you again this soon. Please have a seat."

As Joe and Ginny sat in the two chairs in front of Watkins' desk and Watkins sat back down behind her desk, she continued, "How can I help you?"

"Thank you for agreeing to see us again on such short notice," said Ginny. "We've learned a few things since we were here earlier this week. We think you can help shed some light on some of it."

"I'm more than happy to try."

"But that means you have to be honest and thorough with us," interjected Joe.

"Excuse me. Why did you say that? Do you have reason to think I haven't been so far?"

"Yes, we do," responded Joe as he leaned forward.

"Well, I think I can say the same about you two. Colonel Burke told me that you had told him that Mr. Dalton was killed. Were you ever going to mention it to me?"

"That's part of the reason we're here this morning," said Ginny.

"And the other part of the reason?"

"It turns out we retrieved Mr. Dalton's cell phone around the corner from where he was killed," answered Joe,

"And?"

"And we found several things of interest, but one voice-mail message stood out," said Joe. "It was from a Sergeant Andrews here at Aegis. And he instructed Dalton not to return with his friend for a follow-up interview, but, rather, to meet Colonel Burke at some secluded corner here in Columbus."

"Well, uh, I don't know anything about that call."

"And you didn't instruct Sergeant Andrews to make that call?" asked Joe in a louder than normal voice.

"No, I didn't. In fact, I don't even know any Sergeant Andrews."

"Did Colonel Burke order him to make that call?"

"I have no idea. I surely know nothing about whether or not he did. The colonel doesn't provide me with a report every time he tells someone to do something."

"Has he given you similar instructions in the past related to other people?"

"No, not that I can recall."

"OK. We'd like to speak with Sergeant Andrews. Please ask him to join us."

"Hold on. I need to check the computer for his phone extension." And, a few minutes later, "Detectives, there is no Sergeant Andrews here. In fact, there's no one with that name anywhere in our company."

"That's interesting," said Joe. "Who knew that both Dalton and Meyers were scheduled for a second round of interviews here, after passing the first round? Who could have known that and then possibly been the one who made the call changing things?"

"Well, the colonel and me, and the folks we lined up to conduct the interviews. And, of course, Mr. Dalton himself and his friend, Meyers. And anyone they may have told."

"Is that it?" asked Joe.

"No. Our interview schedule is in the computer and most of our staff here would have access to look at it if they wanted to."

"And does the computer keep track of anyone who does look?"

"Not for this type of information, which isn't really secret or sensitive. The computer does track access to our classified files, but not administrative files like this."

"We need to speak with Colonel Burke again. Will he be back in town in the near future?'

"I have no idea. I can check. If he won't be, should I try to arrange another telephone call?"

"Yes, please," answered Ginny.

"OK. That's it. For now," said Joe. We're heading back to Jasper Creek and we'll expect to hear from you after you've spoken with him."

"Yes, I'll call you."

"OK. Thanks. Good-bye," said Ginny.

"Good-bye."

Joe and Ginny left the offices and headed around the corner to their car. Joe checked his map and headed for South Glenwood Avenue where it passes under the I-70 West Freeway, where Dalton and Burke presumably had met the day of Dalton's murder. After a few blocks of solid high-rise office buildings, the area rapidly changed, first to attractive apartment buildings, and then to garden apartments and private houses. The area then went rapidly downhill from well-kept to rundown to slum-like, with several boarded-up houses and a number of lots, empty except for huge weeds and trash. Soon enough, they reached South Glenwood and the freeway. Joe pulled over and killed the engine. He and Ginny got out of the car and walked around a bit. Other than this being a very deserted and desolate area, the perfect place for meeting someone undetected, they saw nothing of interest. They were soon back in the car and heading to Jasper Creek.

"Well, that visit with Watkins was pretty enlightening," said Ginny.

"Whadda ya think of her reaction to our mentioning the phone call to Dalton?" Joe asked. "So quick to deny knowing anything about it. Too quick, you think?"

"Yes. But assuming she told us the truth, I can't wait to meet or at least talk again with Burke."

"That makes two of us."

"I do think the part about there being no Sergeant Andrews anywhere in Aegis was true. It'd be too easy for us to check. And I don't think Watkins is stupid."

"You and I agree once again. This is getting scary."

Later that afternoon, Watkins called Joe. It turned out that the colonel would be away for a while longer, but he could call the detectives at 11 the next morning. Joe said that 11 o'clock would work and they'd expect the colonel's call then.

Chapter 17

A t exactly 11 a.m. the next day, the phone in the conference room, where Joe and Ginny had been waiting for the call, rang. Joe answered it and put it on speaker.

"Hello, Detective McFarland."

"Good morning, detective. This is Colonel Burke of Aegis Control."

"Good morning, Colonel. I have you on speakerphone and Detective Harris is here with me."

"Good morning, Colonel," said Ginny.

"Good morning, detective. Nicole said that you wanted to speak with me again. What can I help you with?"

"Colonel, we'd like to talk with you about why you had Paul Dalton meet with you in a desolate section of downtown instead of returning to your offices for a second interview. And why you wanted him to keep it a secret from his friend, Alan Meyers."

"What? I don't understand. All I know is that Meyers returned for his interview. But he said that Dalton had some kind of family emergency and he'd reschedule in a few weeks."

"Colonel," said Joe. "We know about the phone call you had Sergeant Andrews make to Mr. Dalton. You might as well tell us why."

"I have no idea what you're talking about. What phone call? And who the heck is Sergeant Andrews?"

"Colonel Burke," said Ginny. "Did you or did you not instruct Sergeant Andrews, or at least someone who said that's who he was, to call Mr. Dalton and tell him that he should not keep his appointment for a second interview with you, but rather he should meet you under one of the I-70 West Freeway overpasses?"

"I most certainly did not."

"Do you know why Ms. Watkins would have arranged such a phone call?"

"No, I don't. Until you mentioned it a minute ago, I didn't even know about such a call."

"Can you think of any reason why she might have arranged it? Or who else might have made or arranged that call?" asked Ginny.

"No idea. I must say that I'm very surprised if what you said is correct. I've not known Ms. Watkins to have ever done anything like that since we've started working together."

"Colonel, when do you expect to be back here? We'd like to meet with you and Ms. Watkins together and iron this out," said Ginny.

"Unless something unexpected comes up, I'm planning to be back next week, on Thursday."

"OK, great. We'll have Ms. Watkins schedule a meeting for the four of us for later that day."

"OK," said Burke. "Is there anything else?"

"No, that's it for now. Thanks for calling us, and we'll see you when you return," concluded Joe.

"OK, good-bye," and the line went dead.

"Well, I think we're finally making some progress," said Ginny.

"Yup, one or both of them is likely lying, or do I have to use the politically correct term, 'has misspoken?' "

" 'Lying' works just fine with me. There's clearly a liar here, perhaps two. Unless one of them has amnesia, or something else is going on that we have no idea of."

"You got that right."

"Joe, as you suggested, let's see if we can figure out why that specific warehouse was chosen for the killing."

"OK. Why don't you try to dig deeper into the building owner? I'll see what I can find by checking out previous tenants of the building. And perhaps also the tenants of other buildings that Pentell owns. But first, why don't you bring the chief up to date? I'm just not up to participating with him and all his friendly banter today."

"Sure. The chief doesn't even know what 'friendly banter' means," said Ginny with a smile.

Joe merely smiled back and nodded as Ginny headed for the chief's office.

"Good morning, Chief. Got time for a quick update on that warehouse killing we're working?"

"Sure, Ginny. Come on in and have a seat."

Ginny brought the chief up to date, highlighting the recently discovered phone message left for Dalton.

"Yeah, I agree with you. One of them may well be lying. Can't wait to hear what happens when you get them both in a room together. It just might throw this case into high gear."

"We're proceeding as fast as we can. Some cases just break faster than others."

"You and I know that, Ginny. But the politicians and

the media folks don't. They want this blot on the image of our fair city wiped away. ASAP."

"We're focused on it, Chief, and doing all we can."

"I know, Ginny. That was meant as a motivating expression of support, not a complaint."

"I know, Chief. And thanks."

"Welcome. Now go catch the S.O.B."

Ginny returned to her desk and suggested that she and Joe have lunch before returning to the case. And to neither's surprise, they quickly found their way around the corner to Sancho's Taco Shop.

Chapter 18

Back at their desks, Ginny began collecting all the information she could gather on Theodore Pentell.

At the same time, Joe focused on the city's and county's online corporate and property records, trying to identify every building that Pentell or his real estate company, JC Realty Investments, owned. He then contacted the city and county tax departments, and asked them to do a computer search of their tax files to identify any and all persons or companies listing their address anytime over the past five years as one of the properties owned by Pentell or JC Realty Investments. Joe wound up with seven buildings and a total of slightly over 200 tenants at some point over the past five years. Of these, approximately 35 were individuals or partnerships, with the remaining almost 175 tenants being corporations.

Joe sloshed through this data best he could, but he soon realized that he could make faster progress if he went to the Ohio Department of Taxation in Columbus. There, he could learn the names of the owners and key executives of each of these companies. Ginny agreed to go there with him the next morning.

Joe spent the rest of the afternoon organizing the various lists he had, hoping that it would make their search the next day that much more efficient. Ginny kept her head focused on her computer monitor, finding and printing numerous articles and facts about Pentell.

By eight the next morning, Joe and Ginny were on the highway, heading once again to Columbus. With some rush hour traffic and a breakfast stop, it was close to 10 by the time they parked their car and walked into the Department of Taxation offices, which were inconveniently located on the northern edge of Columbus.

"Good morning. Ms. Felton please," Joe said to the middle-aged, overweight woman sitting behind the counter.

"I'm Carole Felton. How can I help you?"

"Good morning. I'm Detective McFarland, and this is my partner, Detective Harris. I spoke with you yesterday about needing to get some ownership and key officers information for a bunch of different companies."

"Oh, yes. I remember, detective. Come back here with me. I'll get each of you set up at one of our computer terminals. You should be able to find most of what you're looking for online. For the rest, God help us, if you really need it, you'll have to go over to the annex around the corner and search through our paper files. That could be a monster task."

"Well, let's start with the computerized info and see how far that gets us. If we're lucky, we won't need to make that paper search."

"OK, follow me,"

After getting Joe and Ginny settled in front of the computer terminals, Felton logged them in and searched the first few companies to show them how to do the search and how to print out the information once they found it. She then watched Joe and Ginny each do a couple of searches on their own to be sure they understood how to do it. "OK, looks like you both have this down pat. Go at it. I'll be at the front counter if you need any help. The toilets, as well as the vending and coffee machines, are also out front."

"Thank you for all your help," said Ginny.

Joe and Ginny worked in silence for the next hour.

"Jeez, Ginny, this is tedious as hell. How come the cops on all those TV shows never have to spend hours doing this crap?"

"Yeah, well, welcome to the real world. Let's just hope we find something useful here. I'd really hate having to go to the catacombs around the corner and do all this with the actual paper files."

"You're right about that. At least here we've got comfortable chairs in an air conditioned room and our computer terminals. No heavy lifting required."

And then two hours later, including a timeout for a restroom break and two trips to the candy and coffee vending machines, "Hey, Joe, I think I've got something here."

"Great. What is it?"

"One of the buildings that JC Realty Investments owns is at 423 Worth Street. And one of its tenants for the past two years has been Security Consulting, Inc."

"OK. What's so special about that?"

"Who do you think owns Security Consulting?"

"I have no idea. Elvis?"

"Close. But no. It's a wholly-owned subsidiary of Aegis

Control. Why would they rent space there? And funny that neither Burke or Watkins bothered to mention it to us."

"Yes, it is. I suggest we swing by there and talk to the office manager or whatever on our way back this afternoon."

"I agree. In fact, let's go now. We want to be sure to get there before they close for the day. And it'd be nice to beat rush hour."

"Yeah, and you're as sick of doing this as I am," said Joe.

So they gathered up their papers, thanked Ms. Felton and were soon on their way back to Jasper Creek.

Catching just the leading edge of traffic, Joe and Ginny were back in Jasper Creek a little before 3 o'clock. Joe parked in the street opposite a fire hydrant, pulling down the sun visor to clearly show their PD affiliation. Walking into the lobby of 423 Worth St., the directory of tenants showed that Security Consulting was on the third floor. A slow ride up in the ancient elevator and a walk down the hall to the left got them in front of suite 307. Joe knocked, but no answer. He knocked again, louder. But still no answer.

Ginny, peering through the frosted glass window in the door, said "It doesn't even look like the lights are on, Joe."

"I think you're right, Ginny. Let's check with a few of the neighbors."

Joe and Ginny entered the offices on both sides of suite 307, as well as suite 308, almost directly across the hall. The answers they received were eerily similar. The space had been vacant for several years before Security Consulting apparently had rented it a couple of years earlier. This was based on when their name was stenciled on the door window and added to the directory in the lobby; it was not based on ever seeing anyone enter or leave those offices. The lights also never seemed to be turned on, and they were perfect neighbors — noise or voices were never heard coming from suite 307.

"Very weird," said Ginny. "Either they only work from midnight to 5 a.m., or they never moved into this space. I'll run down to the lobby and see if I can find the building manager or leasing agent so we can get a look at the office space."

"Good idea."

A few minutes later, Ginny was back with a tall, very thin man, probably about 60 years old with his few remaining hairs combed back and forth over his otherwise totally bald head. Mr. Simmons unlocked the door to suite 307. It took only a few minutes for Joe and Ginny to conclude there was nothing useful there. Three rooms each contained a plain metal desk and a simple desk chair. There were no file drawers or cabinets, much less any files. The fourth room had four folding tables arranged in a big rectangle with about 15 chairs around them. The four rooms were clean and totally barren of any office supplies or papers. There were a few telephones plugged in and sitting on the floor. Ginny checked and found there was no dial tone. She made a note in her notebook to check with the phone company to see who had last had phone service. In answer to their question, Simmons said he knew nothing about the tenants. Other than being instructed to put their name in the directory and on the door to the suite a few years earlier, he never saw or heard anything from or about them. He indicated that all the tenants paid their rent directly to Pentell's office. They thanked Simmons, left the suite and were soon on their way back to the PD.

"They clearly never really moved in," said Joe. "Or they'd moved in but have since moved out. Why would they rent this for something like two years and never use it? Even the JC government isn't that inefficient and wasteful."

"I can only think of two reasons," said Ginny. "Either it turned out they didn't need the office but were stuck with a too-expensive-to-cancel lease, or this provides a nice legitimate-looking way to move money to Pentell every month."

"Right on, Ginny. One more thing for us to check on, and figure out which of those explanations is the right one."

Over the following week, things slowed down on the case as Joe and Ginny basically waited for their meeting with Burke. Fortunately, in the interim, they had several other cases and never-ending paperwork to keep them busy. Also, fortunately, the media interest in the case seemed to cool off as time passed. With little or nothing to report, the homicide of Dalton moved further and further back in the newspaper and fell off the TV news shows almost completely. But this didn't stop the chief or Ann Messing from the Prosecutor's Office bugging Joe and Ginny every other day or so, repeatedly pushing for some major progress in solving the murder. Joe and

Ginny calmly reassured the chief and Messing, several times in fact, that they were doing all they could and that progress was being made.

Chapter 19

Finally, the following Thursday rolled around and Joe and Ginny were back at Aegis Control in Columbus. They were immediately escorted into Burke's office. Burke looked like the perfect former special ops officer now running a mercenary firm: tall and well built, with short straight brown hair starting to gray at the temples, complemented by blue eyes, a straight nose and a strong jutting chin. After the formalities of greetings, sitting down and saying no to the coffee offer, Joe began, "Colonel, OK if we get right into things?"

"Most definitely, detective."

"Good. Just for the record, let me ask you again. Is it your position that you had no idea that a Sergeant Andrews, or someone using that name, called Mr. Dalton and left him a message to meet you on the other side of town rather than returning here for his second interview with you? And that he was not to say anything to his friend who was with him?"

"Yes. That's what I told you over the phone. And nothing's changed."

"And you have no idea whether Ms. Watkins was involved in that?"

"That's true, assuming that there was such a call."

"Oh, there was all right. We have Mr. Dalton's phone with the message on it. We'll want to get Ms. Watkins in here to resolve this, but before you call her in, there's one other item we'd like to discuss."

"OK. What is it?"

"Colonel, why does one of Aegis Controls' subsidiaries rent an office in Jasper Creek?" asked Ginny.

"Um, I'm not sure. We have several subsidiaries and many of them have one or more facilities elsewhere. This is really just our corporate headquarters here. None of our subsidiaries work out of here."

"And you don't know which subsidiary is renting Jasper Creek space, much less why?"

"That's true. We can, of course, check our records and get that info. Whoever is renting it, it's not for their main offices. I've been to all of our subsidiaries' main offices, and I know that none of them are in Jasper Creek. But many of them have branch or specialty offices, and that's probably one of them."

"OK," said Ginny. "We can pursue that question later. Now, please ask Ms. Watkins to join us so that we can get to the bottom of that phone message."

"Will do," said Burke as he picked up the phone on his desk, dialed one number and instructed his administrative assistant to have Captain Watkins join them.

Watkins walked in a couple of minutes later. "Hello, Colonel, welcome back. And hello, detectives, good to see you again. What's this about?"

"Have a seat, Nicole," said Burke as he started right in. "Nicole, did you ….?"

"Hold on, Colonel. We'd rather that we do the questioning."

"Uh. OK. Sorry. I was just trying to help."

"We appreciate your intent," said Ginny.

"Let me ask both of you," said Joe. "Were either of you aware of the message left for Mr. Dalton to not return here for his second interview? Did either of you make or arrange that call? Do either of you know a Sergeant Andrews or someone who was using that name?"

"No to all those questions," said Burke.

"Same for me," said Watkins. "Until you told me about it."

"Any ideas as to who might have made that call or been involved with arranging it? Or who the mysterious Sergeant Andrews might be?"

"No," responded Burke and Watkins in unison.

"Any idea why this was done? Why would anyone not want Mr. Dalton to return here? And why have him go to the other side of town thinking he was going to meet the colonel?"

"I have no idea," said Watkins.

"Well, with hindsight, this may have been done somehow in conjunction with his murder. But I'm not sure how it ties in, given that he was killed in Jasper Creek, not in downtown Columbus," offered Burke.

"Let's change the subject for a few minutes. Why does a subsidiary of your firm rent office space in Jasper Creek?" asked Joe.

"As I said earlier, I have no idea. But I'm sure we can check our computer files and have the answer to that pretty quickly," said Burke.

"No need," said Watkins. "I know without looking. I helped negotiate the lease."

"Do you think you could be kind enough to fill the rest of us in?" asked Joe.

"Sure. The space is leased by Security Consulting, Inc. We bought Security Consulting about four years ago and we continue to run it as a separate subsidiary. I helped them find and lease that space a couple of years ago."

"Why, when you have this large office space right here in Columbus?" asked Joe.

"First off, the space here is only our corporate offices. None of our divisions or subsidiaries work out of here. They each have their own main facility and most of them have one or more branch offices."

"Wouldn't it have been more efficient for them to rent space in Columbus?" asked Joe.

"Perhaps, but there's really very little interaction between anyone in our corporate headquarters and anyone in one of the branches of one of our operating divisions or subsidiaries. Especially in this case."

"Why especially in this case?" asked Ginny.

"Security Consulting is the only non-military part of our company. It provides security and security consulting to non-military clients. Like corporations, wealthy business people, show business and sports personalities. That sort of thing."

"And?" asked Joe.

"And, we want to keep it separate from our military security work. Some of its clients don't hold military security contractors in the highest regard. It's not a secret that we own Security, but we don't want to rub it in our clients' faces. And then there's the staffing issues."

"Staffing issues?" asked Joe.

"Our corporate staff and all of our operations except Security Consulting are almost exclusively ex-military, most from special ops. As a result they have top training, are rather straitlaced and focused and are highly paid, in part for the risks they deal with. By comparison, most of the staff at Security Consulting are ex-cops, bodyguards and so on. They're much less trained, less disciplined and not as well paid. We like to keep these two groups of employees from interacting with each other."

"Understood," said Joe. "And what do they use that Jasper Creek office space for?"

"It's often unused. But they do use it for meetings and training. And, occasionally, they bring a client or potential client there for a meeting. These clients prefer to remain anonymous, so those meetings are usually late at night or on weekends, as are the internal meetings and training sessions."

"So that's why no one ever sees them there," said Ginny.

"Yes, I suppose so."

"Why does Security Consulting need this facility in Ohio?" asked Joe.

Burke chimed in. "Security's headquarters are in Miami. They didn't necessarily need space specifically in Ohio, but they needed something in the Northeast."

"That's right," said Watkins. "And when I became aware of that need, I knew there were several buildings not far from Columbus that had vacant space for a number of years and could, therefore, probably be picked up fairly cheaply."

"And how did you find that specific building?" asked Ginny.

"Saw it on an Internet listing by a local broker."

"Makes sense," said Joe. "We'd like to get a copy of the lease agreement as well as the name and contact info of the real estate broker you dealt with."

"No problem," said Watkins.

Noticing just the slightest nod of Ginny's head, Joe continued. "Why didn't either of you mention to us that you, or one of your subsidiaries, lease space in Jasper Creek once you learned that's where we're from?"

"As I said earlier, I wasn't aware of the lease," said Burke.

"And I didn't see the relevance. We lease space all over the country, the world, in fact, and this is one very small, very minor office."

"Understood," said Joe.

Ginny then jumped in. "Back to that phone message left for Mr. Dalton, we'd like to play the message for you now to see if either of you can recognize the voice."

Ginny took out a recorder and played a copy of the voicemail message. Both Burke and Watkins said they didn't recognize the voice.

Joe and Ginny waited while Watkins got a copy of the lease agreement and the real estate broker's business card for them, after which they said their good-byes, retrieved their car and headed back to Jasper Creek.

Once on the highway, Joe said "Maybe we should try to swing by and see the real estate guy before we get back to our desks."

"Good idea. I'll give him a call now." And a few minutes later, Ginny had an appointment for them to meet William Hastings in his office.

"Boy, how did we ever live before cell phones?"

"Yeah," said Ginny. "Remember how you had to keep a pile of coins for pay phones. And after you found one you had to get out of your car regardless of the neighborhood or weather. And, if you were lucky, the phone was in working order,"

"I remember it only too well. And that's what we call the good old days. Not always all that it was cracked up to be."

After parking right in front of the building, Joe and Ginny walked into a real estate office on the ground floor. They told the receptionist that they had an appointment with Mr. Hastings, and a few minutes later they were sitting in a small conference room with him.

"Mr. Hastings," started Ginny, "thanks for seeing us. As I mentioned over the phone, we'd like some information about your involvement in helping Security Consulting, Inc. lease some space on Worth Street a few years ago."

"Yes, I grabbed the file after you called. But I didn't really need it as I remember most of the details."

"Really? What was so special about it?"

"Well, first of all, although our firm handles all kinds of real estate transactions, from office space to warehouses to private residences and even to vacant land, I specialize in industrial and commercial real estate and handle all of those types of transactions for our firm here in the county. And compared to residential work, I typically do fewer, but larger-value deals. That makes it easy to remember many of them. But this one was so strange that I'd remember it anyhow."

"Strange. In what way?" asked Ginny.

"Well normally when I'm representing the buyer or lessee, I first try to understand their needs, I then show them a number of properties and help them decide which one to pursue. After that, I usually play a major, and helpful I might add, role in negotiating the price and terms of the deal."

"And I assume you're saying that wasn't the case with this deal."

"That's right. When Security Consulting, or actually an officer of Aegis Control acting on Security Consulting's behalf, first came to me, they had already selected the property and negotiated the price and terms with the owner of the property. Although I earned my normal commission, I didn't really contribute anything other than shuffling papers. And I warned them about the price."

"What about the price?"

"Well, they had agreed to $15 per square foot, even though the market at that time was more like $8 per square foot. The lady from Aegis Control didn't seem to care when I pointed that out. I guessed that it was for some kind of government contract where they just passed whatever their costs were onto the government. No wonder our taxes are so high!"

"Was that lady Nicole Watkins?" asked Ginny.

"Yes, that's correct."

"Mr. Hastings, are you sure she understood by how much they'd be overpaying and that she didn't seem to care?"

"Yes, exactly."

"Did you get involved in furnishing the offices or helping them move in? Do you know what they use the space for?"

"No, to both those questions."

"Well, that's about it for now," said Ginny. "Thank you for meeting with us and answering our questions. We may be back if we have more questions. Here are our cards. Please call us if you think of anything else."

"OK. Good-bye."

Joe and Ginny left and were soon back at their desks, each with a cup of very stale, very strong coffee.

"Well, that was rather illuminating," said Ginny.

"Yeah, it was. I'm going to try and get hold of the president of Security Consulting and see if he can add anything."

"Good idea, Joe. But how? We don't even know his name."

"Watch and learn."

In short order, searching Google, Joe found the address and phone number of Security Consulting's headquarters in Florida. He called the number, explained that he was a police officer and needed to speak with the president. While waiting, Joe put the call on his speaker so that Ginny could hear both sides of the conversation.

About two minutes later, "Hello, this is Charles Foster. Is everything all right? My wife? My daughters?"

"Yes, Mr. Foster. Sorry to have frightened you. As far as we know, everything is fine with your family. I'm calling on another matter. I'm with the Jasper Creek, Ohio, police department."

"Ohio? What's this about?"

"Mr. Foster, we're trying to learn some details about the office space you rent here in Jasper Creek."

"Yes, we rent a few offices there. What do you want to know?"

"How did you pick Jasper Creek?"

"We didn't."

"Can you explain that a little more fully?"

"Yes, sure. The strategic plan we put together shortly after Aegis Control acquired us included plans to open four or five branch offices across the country. Soon after the planning meetings at corporate, I was called by Nicole Watkins. She's the head of administration at Aegis."

"Yes, we've met Ms. Watkins. Please continue."

"Surprisingly to me, she told us that she had found the perfect place for us and she had already negotiated a lease for it. All we had to do was sign the lease. She said that Colonel Burke would be impressed with how quickly we were starting to actually implement our plan."

"And then?"

"Well, I signed the lease. Ms. Watkins helped get us the little furniture we needed. And we occasionally use the space and, of course, pay the rent each month."

"We got the sense that the space isn't used all that much."

"That's true. It turns out that most of our business has developed on the West Coast and in the South, with little growth in the Northeast. Looks like we moved too fast on the lease. The lease still has about eight years to go, and it would be extremely expensive to terminate it early."

"One other question, Mr. Foster. Did Ms. Watkins help you with any of your other office leases?"

"No, she didn't. Just that one in Ohio."

"OK, thank you, Mr. Foster. You've been very helpful. Have a nice day."

"You're most welcome. And same to you."

"Well done, Joe. Looks like Ms. Watkins has won a ticket for another meeting with us."

"Yes it does. But it's time to call an end to today."

"You're right about that. But we can't see Watkins tomorrow as we have that all-day terrorism training session."

"Yeah. Shows how screwed up this world has become that we need to spend a full day on that."

"I agree, Joe. But, sadly, it is important that we stay on top of the latest techniques."

"No question. We'll have to be about halfway to Cincinnati by eight. No point in our taking two cars. How about I pick you up at six? That'll give us time for a gourmet breakfast at a McDonald's along the way."

"Sounds like a plan. I'll see you at six. Have a good night's sleep."

"Thanks. You too, Ginny."

A few minutes later, they were both out of PD headquarters, in their cars and driving home.

Chapter 20

The next morning, Joe was sitting in his car in front of Ginny's apartment 15 minutes before six. At five minutes before six, Ginny walked up to Joe's car and got in. They were quickly on I-70, where they exited as soon as they saw the first sign for a McDonald's. Following two Egg McMuffins and coffee for Joe and pancakes and coffee for Ginny, they were back on I-70 and then I-75. They reached the training site 20 minutes early. They enjoyed freshly brewed coffee and doughnuts as they roamed around the meeting room and met several other officers from police departments throughout the western half of Ohio.

The course, taught by instructors from Homeland Security and the FBI, was much more interesting and useful than either Joe or Ginny had expected. It included both classroom lectures and simulated exercises, and covered everything — terrorist bomb attacks, attacks at schools and malls, so-called lone-wolf terrorist activities and everything in between. The attendees were given many tips on what to do, and not do, in various circumstances and whom to call for more help in which situations.

Joe and Ginny were back on the highway toward Jasper Creek by a little after four.

"Wanna grab some dinner?" asked Joe.

"Sure. What do you have in mind?"

"You'll see. I'm gonna surprise you. You head home, relax or whatever. I'll pick you up at 7:30."

"Well, this sounds quite intriguing. At least tell me how I should dress. How fancy?"

"Nothing fancy. Pants and a shirt are fine. Now, no more questions. You'll find out after I pick you up."

Joe and Ginny spent the rest of the car ride talking about all they had heard and seen during the day. They hoped they'd never need to use what they had learned, but agreed that it was reassuring to know what to do just in case.

Ginny got home and was thankful that she had enough time for a nice soaking in her tub. This was one of Ginny's most enjoyable activities. Unfortunately, her work rarely provided sufficient time for a long soak, other than on her days off. While soaking, she couldn't stop thinking about how her relationship with Joe seemed to be taking a different, and pleasant, turn. Ginny was still too unsure of the future to let herself dare to dream about a life together with Joe. She felt that she was ready to make such a commitment, but she doubted that Joe was. She knew that Joe liked her, definitely as a partner and friend, and most likely also in a more romantic way. But she wasn't sure how strong his feelings about her were. Nor was she at all sure that he was ready to proceed to the next level, given his fear of being hurt again. She was well aware how the death of his wife and son damn near destroyed him, and only now was he starting to truly recover from the accident 11 years earlier. Nonetheless, Joe's invitation to dinner, which seemed to be a spontaneous act, was a big step forward. Ginny closed her eyes for a few minutes, trying to imagine life with Joe. Then she brought herself back to reality, opened the drain and climbed out of the tub. Next it was on to drying, hairdo, makeup and clothes. Ginny was all ready and sitting in her living room at 7:10.

Joe had no time for a leisurely bath. He was as surprised as Ginny was when he had invited her to dinner. It was as if his subconscious issued the invitation without discussing it with him first. In a way, Joe was glad it had happened that way. He knew that if he had thought about and analyzed it first, he most likely wouldn't have invited her. He liked her well enough; that wasn't the question. It was more a fear of messing up their current partner and best friend relationship, as well as of one or both of them getting badly hurt if the relationship developed and then something were to happen.

Joe chuckled to himself; for a big, strong, grown-up detective, he sure had a lot of fears. Joe decided that he was going to cook dinner. He used to do this quite often with his wife, Lori, and he had developed into a pretty good cook. In fact, Lori used to teasingly refer to him as "Chef Joseph." But since her death, he hadn't cooked anything more exotic than scrambled eggs or burgers on the grill. Unless you considered heating frozen dinners in the microwave to be exotic cooking.

On his way home, Joe stopped at the local liquor store where he picked up a bottle of California cabernet sauvignon and a six-pack of imported Belgian beer. He wanted to be ready whether Ginny preferred wine or beer. He then headed to the supermarket, where he gathered up two sirloin steaks, assorted fresh salad items and vegetables, a handful of different spices and sauces and an oven-ready garlic bread. Joe drove home, took a quick shower and changed into clean clothes. He cut the steaks into small cubes, left them to marinate in one of the sauces he had purchased and prepared a salad. Then he was on his way to pick up Ginny.

During the 15-minute ride to Ginny's apartment, Joe felt like a teenage boy about to embark on his first real date. He had been to Ginny's apartment several times, but, except for the recent visit when Ginny had the flu, it almost always had been to pick her up or drop her off before or after work. He'd even had morning toast and coffee or an after-work beer or two there several times. But this was different. Joe parked in the visitors' parking area behind the garden apartments where Ginny lived. Up the steps to the second floor and he was in front of Ginny's door. He rang the bell. When she opened the door, his mouth dropped open. Ginny looked so fresh and clean and happy. It was as if this was the first time that he had ever really seen her. Ginny wasn't beautiful in the traditional sense, but she was quite attractive and had a nice, trim figure. She had a smile that radiated enough happiness to spread to anyone else in the room with her. Joe put his hands on her shoulders, leaned in and kissed her softly on her mouth. Ginny kissed him back. After a few seconds, they broke apart and headed down the steps and outside to Joe's car.

"OK, sir. *Now* can you tell me where you're taking me to dinner?"

"Nope. You'll just have to wait and see for yourself."

Picking up on the route Joe was taking, Ginny quickly surmised that they were going to Joe's house. But, not wanting to ruin Joe's surprise, and just in case she was wrong, she said nothing. Only when they got to within a few blocks of Joe's house, Ginny asked "Joe, are we going to your house?"

"Wow, you sure are a great detective. Well done. And yes, we are going to my house. I plan to show you how a real chef cooks dinner."

"I'm impressed already."

Ginny also had been to Joe's several times, but only for a cup of coffee or a beer; the coffee on the way to a crime scene or to interview a witness or suspect and, late in the day, a beer on the way back. Joe's house was a single-floor bungalow, with a living room/dining room combination, a compact kitchen, two bedrooms, one of which Joe had converted into a combination office and exercise room, and a bathroom. The house was small and simply furnished. It was clean, with everything put away. Knowing Joe, Ginny was sure that it had been this way and was not put into shape that evening just for her visit.

What followed was a delightful dinner. Joe wouldn't let Ginny help with any of the preparation or cooking. Ginny sat at the kitchen table while "Chef Joseph" did his thing. They were through four beers and a third of the bottle of wine by the time they sat down for dinner. The meal was tasty and nicely presented. Ginny was very impressed and repeatedly told Joe so. Joe did let Ginny help with the dishes, after which they sat in the living room and finished the last two beers and the remaining wine.

"That was delicious, Joe. And very enjoyable. Thank you so much."

"Yeah. I enjoyed it too. Now it's time to close up shop. It's getting late, and you need your beauty sleep."

"Yes. Sad but true. Although we have the whole weekend to get as much sleep as we want. But now, I'm sorry to say, you have to drive me back home. If this wasn't such a surprise, I could have driven here and saved you the trip now."

"Very true. But I have a much better idea."

"What's that?" asked Ginny, with a small smile breaking out on her face.

"Well, since we don't have to worry about anyone seeing your car here overnight, and since it's important to do our share for the planet by avoiding unnecessary driving, why not spend the night here?"

"Oh, Joe, you are so practical and such a devoted environmentalist."

So Ginny did spend the night at Joe's. But this time, they did more than just sleep together. In fact, Ginny remained there until Monday morning. They never left the house, except for Joe making a Saturday afternoon run back to the liquor store and supermarket.

Chapter 21

Joe and Ginny were up early on Monday as they wanted to get to Watkins' office by nine. While having toast and coffee in Joe's kitchen, they looked and felt like two teenagers who had snuck off and had sex without their parents finding out.

"Joe, I can't begin to tell you how great this weekend was. After all these years, I feel like I was born again. No, not in a religious sense!"

"I know what you mean. Uh, the sex was great, but it was more than that. I truly feel like you and I have finally totally connected with each other. Yeah, sure, we've been partners and good friends for quite a while, but this is much more."

"No question." And, with her cheeks turning bright pink, she added, "We had much more sex this weekend than most partners and friends do. Just kidding, Joe. This really was very special for me. I'm not sure what it all means, or where it might lead, but, for now, I'm floating on a cloud."

"I think I'm on the same cloud as you. But now we need to climb down, get into my car and head off to see our good friend Captain Watkins in Columbus."

At Ginny's request, Joe made a quick detour to Ginny's apartment. Ten minutes later, having changed into a fresh set of clothing and applied her basic makeup, Ginny was back in Joe's car.

En route to Columbus, their conversation naturally turned to their upcoming visit with Watkins.

"Do you think she'll be surprised to see us?" asked Ginny.

"Yes, I do. That's why I didn't want us to call and schedule an appointment. This way, she may not have thought through a whole BS story."

"What if she refuses to talk?"

"Well, if she lawyers up, we're of course done. But if she just refuses, we can threaten to be back in a couple of hours with a warrant, at which point she'd have to come with us to Jasper Creek for questioning."

"Yeah, I'm sure she'd rather just have a quiet talk in her office instead of us escorting her out of Aegis."

"That's what we're counting on."

Joe and Ginny were sitting in the Aegis lobby a little after 8:30. When Watkins walked in about 15 minutes later, she was clearly surprised to see them sitting there.

"Detectives. Good morning. I didn't expect to see you this morning. Are you here to see me? How can I help you?"

"We need to speak with you," said Joe.

"Uh, fine. Let's go to my office," said Watkins as she led them to her office, closed the door and invited them to sit down. "OK, what's up?"

"This time we'd like the truth. The whole truth," said Joe.

"What do you mean? I've told you the truth."

"Not quite," said Ginny. "We'd like to talk about the Jasper Creek office space leased by Security Consulting."

"OK. What would you like to know?" asked Watkins as some of the color left her cheeks.

"Is it true that you identified that specific office space, and that you negotiated the price and lease terms?" asked Joe.

"Well, yes. That's part of my job as head of administration. To help our operating divisions and subsidiaries with things like that."

"We understand that you did this without Security Consulting asking for your help."

"Yes and no."

"What does that mean?" asked Joe.

"They had stated their need for space like that in their strategic plan. And rather than waiting to be asked, I saw an area where I could be helpful so I proactively proceeded. Anything I can do to keep them focused on their operating objectives rather than administrative stuff is value added to the corporation."

"And why did you negotiate such a long-term lease without any way to terminate the lease early."

"That was our negotiating strategy to get the lowest possible monthly lease rate."

"Oh," said Joe. "You mean a rate that's only twice as high as what the market rates were?"

"I'm sorry, detective. I'm not sure what you're getting at or implying."

"I'm pretty sure you know exactly what we're getting at."

"Before I answer that or any other questions, I want to exercise my right to have my lawyer present."

"I don't blame you," said Ginny. "But no need. We're done for now. Just be sure not to leave the area without contacting us first."

"Thanks for your time," said Joe. "No need to show us out, we know the way."

And with that, Joe and Ginny stood up, left Aegis and headed back to Jasper Creek.

"Joe, when we get back, we need to dig further into the backgrounds of both Watkins and her friendly lessor, Pentell."

"Most definitely."

Chapter 22

After stopping at Sancho's Taco Shop for a quick lunch, Joe and Ginny were back at their desks. Ginny focused on Watkins while Joe spent his time looking into Pentell's background.

At around 3:30, Ginny asked, "Ready to compare notes yet?"

"Sure. I've just about run out of places to look anyhow. You start."

"OK. Turns out there's a bit more to Watkins than we were aware of."

Just then Joe's phone rang.

"Detective McFarland."

"Hey, Joe. This is Ann Messing. How're you doing?"

Joe recognized the assistant prosecutor's voice right away and tried to detect any hints of impatience in it as she asked about the case. "Just great. What can we do for you, Ann?"

"My boss needs an update on where you are with that vacant warehouse homicide. And, of course, he needs it today."

"Not a problem. Why don't you come over now? We also have to give our chief an update. Maybe we can kill two birds with one stone."

"Why, Joe. That's so sweet. This is the first time all day today that I've been called a dead bird."

"Well, that's the kind of gentleman I am."

"OK. OK. I'll be there in about 15 minutes."

Twenty minutes later, Joe and Ginny were sitting in the conference room with the chief and Ann Messing sitting across the table from them. Joe and Ginny brought their guests up to speed, summarizing all they knew, and didn't know, up through their visit with Watkins earlier that day.

"Since we got back here, we've been spending the afternoon digging further into the backgrounds of Watkins and Pentell, the owner of the vacant building. We haven't even had a chance to fill each other in on what we've uncovered."

"OK," said the chief. "Lay it all out now. We'll all learn something together."

Joe and Ginny looked at each other and Joe gave a nod to Ginny.

"OK. I'll start," said Ginny. "I've been digging into Captain, or rather, ex-Captain Watkins, while Joe's becoming an expert on Pentell, the owner of the company that owns not only the vacant building where the vic was found but also the building here in town where Aegis' subsidiary rents offices at twice the going rental rate."

"Go for it, detective," said Messing.

"Well, it turns out that Watkins grew up in the New York City area. She actually worked as a paramedic on Long Island for a few years before she joined the Army. Her paramedic work surely would have made her familiar with propofol, the drug that was used to knock the victim, Dalton, out cold."

"Interesting, but not much I can do with that in court," said Messing.

"Hey, we're just bringing you up to speed with where we are and what we know," interjected Joe. "We didn't call and invite you here because we thought we had the case locked up. You're the one who called us to get an update. Remember?"

"You're right. Sorry. I'm just anxious to see this move ahead and get solved."

"So are all of us," said the chief. "Go ahead, continue, Ginny."

"OK. Thanks, Chief. Turns out that Watkins has a clean military record. Never saw any combat, but performed well and advanced on schedule up to captain. She held a few different positions, but the one of most interest is the 30 months she spent doing administrative work in Germany."

"Why's that so interesting?" asked Messing.

"We learned earlier, and I'm sure Joe will elaborate when I give him the microphone, that Pentell was also stationed in Germany at the same time. In fact they were both in the same logistics brigade over there. They didn't work directly with each other, but it's very probable that they got to know each other over there."

"That is interesting. Good work, Ginny," said the chief. "Anything else on Watkins before Joe takes center stage?"

"Not really. Married and divorced while doing her paramedic thing. Been single ever since. She resigned from the Army in 2008, hooked up with Colonel Burke at Aegis Control a few months after that and, as they say, 'everything else is history.' A few people mentioned rumors of she and Burke having had and maybe still having an affair, but nothing definitive to confirm or deny that. Joe, want to fill us in on Pentell?"

"Sure. As he had told Ginny and me when we first met him, he was in the Army from 1998 to 2006. Other than basic training, he spent his whole time in Germany. He became head of a logistics brigade in Heidelberg, responsible for purchasing and storing and moving equipment and supplies, everything from tanks to toothpaste. It turns out that Watkins worked for one of his section chiefs so they must have known each other. Seems like it was boring, straightforward work, ensuring that our soldiers had all the clothing, equipment and food they needed while serving over there. Nothing else of note to report. He left the service in 2006 and got into the local real estate business, dealing with industrial and commercial buildings, but nothing on the residential side. He married his high school sweetheart when he got out of the Army. They've lived in Jasper Creek and have two young children. But they've been separated for about two years. The wife and kids live in the house. He rented a condo a couple of miles from their house."

"So are we saying that all we have is that Pentell and Watkins probably knew each other in Germany? Not exactly solid proof of committing a homicide," said Messing.

"We know that," said Ginny. "In fact, this may tie more closely to her arranging that long-term lease from Pentell at twice the market rate than it does to the homicide. And we don't even know if that lease is a crime or is in any way related to the homicide. But besides the fact that they knew each other in Germany, it's interesting that neither of them mentioned that to us."

"So what's next?" asked Messing. "My boss is going to be less than ecstatic about the so-called progress we've made so far."

"Take it easy, Ann," said the chief. "Sounds like Joe and Ginny are doing all the right things. Some cases just take longer to unravel than others."

"You're right, Chief. I apologize. I'm just letting my frustrations show."

"Apology accepted," said Ginny. "Our next step is to follow up with Watkins and Pentell to try to figure out why the extra-expensive lease. Embezzlement or black-mail or just stupidity or who knows?"

"Yeah," said Joe. "And, hopefully, it ties in somehow with the homicide. Otherwise, we're still virtually at the starting point on that."

"Well, thanks for the update. The loud noise you'll probably hear in a little while will be my boss cutting me a new one because of our lack of progress."

"That's too bad, Ann. If it will help, have him call me."

"OK, Chief, thanks. It may turn out that these two have nothing to do with the killing. As Ginny said, it may just be plain old embezzlement, but without some hard evidence, it's almost impossible to prove it was embez-zlement rather than just a poorly negotiated lease. Let's hope we get a break on the homicide soon," said Messing as the meeting ended and everyone went back to their own area.

Chapter 23

The next morning, Joe and Ginny were waiting at Pentell's offices when he arrived.

"Good morning, detectives. Did we have a meeting scheduled for this morning?"

"No," said Joe. "But we need to talk with you about something that came up."

"OK. Come on into my office."

After turning down an offer of coffee and sitting in the same chairs as on their first visit, Joe started right in. "You need to tell us everything about your relationship with Nicole Watkins."

With slightly pink cheeks, Pentell asked, "What do you mean?"

"You know exactly what we mean," said Ginny. "And we want everything. Start with your time in Germany."

"Well, OK. But there wasn't really a relationship. She was the administrative support for one of my subordinates. So we knew each other. We occasionally spoke, but it was usually just 'Good morning' or something about work. That was it."

"So nothing personal between you two over there?"

"Heavens no. That would have been totally inappropriate. I mean, we were both single at the time, but still, I was her boss's boss."

"And what about when you two returned to the U.S.?" asked Ginny.

"I left Germany before her, and I had no idea when she left or where she settled back in the States. We had no contact for five or six years."

"And then?" asked Joe.

"Well this is a bit embarrassing."

"Tell us anyhow," said Joe.

"We bumped into each other in a bar in Columbus a few years ago. We started talking, mostly reminiscing about Germany. We agreed to meet a week later for dinner, and things sort of developed from there."

"Sort of developed?" asked Ginny.

"Well, Nicole, er Captain or Ms. Watkins, is single, very attractive and an interesting and impressive person. And I was already separated from my wife."

"So Ms. Watkins didn't play a role in you and your wife separating."

"No, not at all. We were already separated and, in fact, planning to divorce before Nicole and I, er, got together."

"And how would you describe your relationship with Ms. Watkins?" asked Ginny.

"Nothing official, but we're pretty serious. I mean, we've discussed getting married once I'm divorced."

"So that explains it," said Joe.

"Explains what?" asked Pentell.

"Why she arranged a lease with you for one of Aegis' subsidiaries with the rent being twice the market rate."

"OK, we're done here. I've tried to be helpful to you, but ... Nicole told me about your questioning her about this same subject. I'm afraid you'll need to talk with my lawyer if you want to discuss this further."

"That's your right, of course. But it sure doesn't make

you look very innocent. Be sure not to leave town without talking to us first," said Joe.

Joe and Ginny left Pentell's office and went back to theirs. Ginny called Messing and filled her in. Then, while Joe was bringing the chief up to date, Ginny typed up her notes while everything was still fresh in her mind.

"Well that piece of the puzzle is pretty clear," said Ginny. "Intentionally arranging for your employer to pay extra high rent to a landlord, who happens to be your boyfriend and future husband, is a pretty nice way to hide your embezzlement activities."

"Yes, it is. And it was done in a way that Aegis would most likely never uncover what was going on. No one would ever question that relatively unimportant lease, much less realize that the rental rate was excessive. But it was not done in a way good enough to get past us two super sleuths," said Joe.

"Very true. But, we're unfortunately still no place with the homicide. We do have a pretty good case for embezzlement so far. Ann and her boss can decide whether or when to pursue that crime. But like us, I'm sure they're still much more interested in the homicide."

"You can bet on that. And that's the crime you and I have to focus on and solve."

"You got that right, Joe. Let's go back to the conference room and start from the beginning, laying out all the possibilities on the whiteboard."

"Good idea."

With their cups of reheated, hours-old coffee in hand, Joe and Ginny settled into the conference room. Ginny was at the board with a marker in her free hand. Joe was in one of the chairs, leaning back on its two rear legs while his left leg was sprawled on the table in front of him.

"OK, Ginny. Let's start by listing the cast of characters of this drama."

"OK." Ginny rattled off names as she wrote them on the board. "Paul Dalton — the vic, his friend Alan Meyers, Colonel Burke, Watkins, and Pentell. That's about it."

"Just for completeness, let's add the vic's wife, Kristi, and the unknown Sergeant Andrews who left the voice-mail message for Dalton."

"Agreed," said Ginny as she added these two names to the list. "Anyone else?"

"Don't think so. At this point, let's not clutter the board, or our little brains, with minor characters like Meyers' mother or the president of the Security Consulting subsidiary of Aegis."

"OK. What next?"

"Well, although any of these folks could be involved, I'm pretty sure that there has to be something specific between Dalton and Pentell."

"Yup, I think you got that one right, Joe. Unless this was a truly random homicide, and it's way too early to reach that conclusion, there's something about Dalton — who he is, what he did or saw or where he was — that resulted in him becoming the victim."

"Exactly. And the same goes for Pentell. It's pretty unlikely that the victim wound up and was killed in one of his buildings just by chance. That building is far off the beaten track, especially for an out-of-stater like Dalton."

"Yeah, especially since Dalton was supposedly spending all his time in Columbus."

"Good point."

"OK, time to dig in further on these two. Who do you want, Joe?"

"As the kid on our team, why don't you take Dalton? I'll take old-man Pentell."

"Sounds like a plan, Grandpa."

Joe headed back to his desk, after stopping for a refill of even older coffee. After copying down on her pad the names she had written on the board, Ginny followed in Joe's footsteps.

Chapter 24

By mid-afternoon, Joe and Ginny were ready to fill each other in on what they had learned about Pentell and Dalton.

"OK, Joe, you go first. Age before beauty."

"Shucks, I was hoping to go first because of both age and beauty."

"Well one out of two ain't bad," said Ginny with a smile.

"Fair enough. As he wasn't in special ops or any covert activities, I was able to learn a fair amount about Pentell's military service. What he told us pretty well checked out. He did spend almost all of his time in Germany, all of it in a support role. But there were a few things he neglected to mention."

"Aha. Go for it. I'm all ears."

"Well, for one, it was rumored that he and Watkins were screwing around together in Germany. No one had any proof or firsthand knowledge of this, but it was widely rumored throughout the group he supervised."

"And to quote that great philosopher, Joseph McFarland, where there's smoke there's sex."

"Did I really say that?" asked Joe.

"Fraid so. What else?"

"Turns out there were three instances of missing rifles and ammunition under Pentell's watch. Nothing was ever proven and no one was ever officially accused, but the shortages were real."

"Um, interesting. Think he was stealing and selling them?"

"No idea. But it's as good a theory as any."

"What else you got?"

"Not much. His description of his real estate business seems correct, and, unless they were super secretive, his affair back here with Watkins didn't start until after he and his wife were separated."

"Yeah, well I'll keep an open mind as to whether that's true or they were just real good at sneaking around."

"Good. Skepticism makes for good detective work."

"I'll add that to the book I'm writing someday of famous Joseph McFarland sayings."

"Fair enough. What did you pick up on Watkins?"

"Not much more than we already knew. As a very attractive, some would say sexy, lady who never remarried after her short marriage back in her paramedic days, people had her paired up with several different people. The most commonly expressed one being the good Colonel Burke."

"Well, that's just a natural rumor. Just like I'm sure many people think that a sexy lady like you is involved with me."

"Joe! People don't think that, do they?"

"I don't really know, but it wouldn't surprise me. You are a pretty and sexy lady, unattached and spending most of your waking hours with unattached me."

"Jeez, I hate rumors like that."

"Yeah, well, if we continue along our new relationship, we'll go public at some point and then the rumors will become known facts."

"OK, Joe, let's table that for a more private time. Let's focus on the case."

"Yes, ma'am. I was just saying."

"Well, if Watkins is having an affair with Pentell, which seems to be the case, that could explain the high rent payments. But unless she can function on very little sleep, that sort of kills the affair-with-Burke rumor."

"Yeah, and neither explains Dalton's killing."

"Unless Dalton somehow found out about their embezzlement scheme and they killed or had him killed. But why in Pentell's building here in Jasper Creek?"

"Good points, Ginny. Pentell or Watkins, or both, would view killing Dalton in one of Pentell's buildings as an unnecessary risk. And, anyhow, it would be pretty unlikely that Dalton would find out about the embezzlement scheme."

"OK. So where are we? Or aren't we?"

"For one thing, there's clearly a relationship between Watkins and Pentell. One that started either way back in Germany or only when they were both back here."

"Correct. And there also may be, or may have been, a relationship between Watkins and Burke."

"She's one busy lady," concluded Joe.

"Yes," said Ginny. "At a minimum, she's embezzling money from her employer, and possible past or present lover, for her current boyfriend and possible future husband. And we shouldn't totally rule out the possibility that the vic stumbled into some or all of this and was killed to keep him quiet."

"Maybe, but pretty unlikely that he'd get wind of any of this."

"I agree. But what else can it be?"

"Not sure," said Joe. "But I have a gut feeling it's somehow related to the Army. Pentell and Watkins served together, Burke, and in fact almost all of Aegis, is ex-military. And, at about the same time, Dalton was in the service, in fact in Special Ops just like Burke was. No idea what that all means, but the Army's about the only common thread we have."

"You've got a much better understanding of the military stuff than I do. Why don't you dig around that? In the meantime, I'll try to learn more about the mysterious, non-existent Sergeant Andrews and why our vic wound up in an empty warehouse in Jasper Creek."

"Sounds like a plan. But what say we call it a day and start off fresh tomorrow morning?"

"Sounds like an even better plan."

Five minutes later, Joe and Ginny left HQ. Joe dropped Ginny off at her apartment after they both agreed that they needed a night alone to catch up on their sleep if for no other reason.

Chapter 25

Ginny was impressed when she pulled into the small parking lot behind PD HQ at about 7:45 the next morning. Joe's car was already there. Upstairs, Joe was at his desk with papers spread out all over the desk and floor around Joe's chair.

"Well, you look like you've been here quite a while already. Trying to get a promotion?"

"I've been awake since three. I couldn't stop my mind from exploring all the possible military aspects of this case. So I finally just got up and came on in."

"I understand. Any brainstorms yet?"

"No, not yet. But I haven't given up."

"OK. I'll stop distracting you. I'll get a cup of coffee for me and, presumably, another refill for you and then I'll get to work as well."

A few minutes later, Ginny was back with two cups of coffee and was soon at her desk opposite Joe's.

Joe was again reviewing the sheet he had put together, showing for each of the so-called key players when they had been in the service, where they had been stationed and what roles they had played.

About half an hour later, Joe interrupted Ginny. "Hey, Ginny, can I pull you away from your important and exciting work for a couple of minutes? We might find some useful data points if we review this together."

"OK, sure. Go for it."

"Let me make a copy of this for you. Then we can talk it through together."

Joe was back in two minutes, handed the copy to Ginny and started right in.

"I'm trying to find commonalities among all our various military folks. So here goes. Pentell was in the Army from '98 to 2006. After basic training, he spent his entire time in Heidelberg, Germany, in charge of a logistics brigade over there. His stay included three instances of missing guns and ammo. No one knows for sure whether these were thefts, honest misplacements or just bookkeeping screwups. He also had Watkins working for one of his subordinates for part of his time in Germany, and there were unsubstantiated rumors of the two of them having an affair.

"Watkins was in the Army from 2000 to 2008. After basic training and a short stint as a medic, she spent the rest of her time in administrative roles, including the 30 months as an aide to one of Pentell's subordinates in Heidelberg. She allegedly only met Pentell again five years later in a bar in Columbus, and they're now planning marriage after his divorce is final.

"Burke, before starting and running Aegis, was in the Army for 30 years, most of it in the Rangers. He was in charge of a special ops group, but we have no indication that he and Dalton knew each other. He left the Army in 2010 and started Aegis soon thereafter.

"Our vic, Dalton, was in the Army from 2000 to 2009, most of it in Special Ops. And his buddy, Meyers, had the same Army career. He was in the same location as Dalton, but on a different Special Ops team."

"OK, I see all that, Joe. So basically, except for his buddy, Meyers, Dalton had nothing to do with any of the others in the service, unless he saw or heard something."

"Correct. So that could be his only involvement. But the other three could have crossed paths with each other. In fact, we know that Pentell and Watkins did — in Germany. I need to try to find out if Pentell and Burke had any history together."

"Good summary, Joe. But where does that all leave us?"

"Let's see. We've got the following connections. Pentell and Watkins were in Germany together and knew each other for 30 months there, and may or may not have had an affair over there. Dalton and Meyers were in Special Ops at the same location, although on different teams, for several years. And Burke was in charge of a Special Ops group that may have included one or both of their teams. Burke's and Pentell's Army years overlapped, but they were in different groups and different locations."

"And, therefore?"

"Haven't figured that out yet. But I think there's something buried in this pile of connections."

"Probably right. Too many connections to all be coincidental. But I'm not sure how we proceed."

"Me neither. So let's proceed to lunch."

"Splendid idea, detective. A couple of burritos may be just what's needed to stimulate our brain cells."

Joe and Ginny walked around the corner and were soon sitting in their usual booth. Two burritos for Joe, one for Ginny, Diet Cokes for both and a plate of nachos with spicy salsa while they waited for their burritos.

"Ginny, when we get back to our desks, why don't you

keep trying to find out how or why the vic wound up in that warehouse. This is a tough question to answer, but it's a critical one."

"Will do. And you?"

"I'm going to call my Army friend in D.C. to see if there is any record of dealings between our cast of characters. He won't divulge any classified stuff, but he might give me a couple of hints that no one else in the Army's been willing to. After the call, I'll join you on the why-that-warehouse question."

"Works for me. But can we talk about something else?"

"Sure, just name it."

"I'll give you a hint. It's spelled 'U-S.' "

"Yeah, what about the U.S.? A great country, but…."

"No, you dingbat. Not the U.S., us. Us as in Joe and Ginny."

"Oh, gotcha. What do you want to talk about? Things are pretty darn good from my viewpoint."

"Yeah, mine, too. And that's the issue."

"Huh?"

"Well, first off, I'm worried that something this good can't last. Also, I'm not sure how this evolved so suddenly, and, more to the point, where it all may be leading."

"OK, I understand. But I don't have any more answers than you. We need to talk this through."

"Exactly my point. But obviously not here in the restaurant. How about after work, we really make a focused effort to try to figure all this, or at least part of it, out?"

"Works for me. Looks like we have a date for this evening."

"Good. Thanks for humoring me. But now we better pay the bill and mosey on back to work."

Back at their desks, each with a cup of stale, but hot, coffee, Joe rummaged through the pile of business cards in his top desk drawer, picked up the phone and called his Army buddy in Washington.

"Hiya, Bill. You still riding roughshod over that same desk in the Pentagon?"

"Who is this?"

"McFarland. Who the hell do you think it is, the president?"

"Joe. You son of a you-know-what. How've you been? It's been what, two or three years, since we spoke?"

"Yeah. Way too long. And I'm sure my list of excuses is at least as good as yours."

"Probably right. So let's skip that part. Doing OK? Getting over the accident?"

"Yeah. Of course I can't forget it and I think of them very often, but I've been able to move my life along some."

"Glad to hear it. I'm sure you're not calling to invite me to dinner, although we do need to get together one of these days. So you must be calling 'cause you want something from me."

"Bill, you got that right. And, of the two of us, I was supposed to be the detective."

"Well, I guess I know you too well. What can I do for you?"

"We're in the middle of a homicide investigation here. And the vic and most of the others who might be involved were in the Army, in the same place at the same time in a number of cases."

"And?"

"And I need your help in finding out what kinds of dealings they had with each other in the service, any reported incidents that might be helpful to know and so on. A few of them were in Special Ops, and you know how free the Army is with that type of info."

"Glad to see you've retained your perfect record of never asking me for anything easy."

"Yeah, well, I keep the tough requests for the tough folks."

"Joe, I'm happy to try to help, as you knew I'd be. I should be able to cut through some of the Army bureaucracy, but you know I won't disclose anything confidential."

"I wouldn't expect you to, Bill. Let me fax you the names and bits of Army info I have so you can hunt around."

"OK. Same fax number as a few years ago. I'm sure you have it on my tattered business card buried someplace in your desk. How soon do you need whatever I can find?"

"Yesterday would be right on time."

"Gotcha. Give me a day or two and I'll get back to you. But you'll owe me for this. This will definitely put the onus on you to arrange a get-together for the two of us."

"Works for me. And thanks."

"You're welcome. I'll call you in a day or two. Bye."

"So long."

Ginny, who had been listening to Joe's side of the telephone conversation, said, "Sounds like that was a smart call to make."

"Yeah. If it's there, Bill will find it. If it's confidential, he won't give me the info, but he'll provide a few hints. He's a good guy and a good friend."

"From your days in the service?"

"Yeah, we served together. And worked closely with each other on Army tasks as well as when on leave."

"OK. I won't ask you the details of those activities while you were on leave. Now that I'm done eavesdropping on your call, let's start trying to figure out how and why our vic wound up in a deserted warehouse here in JC."

Joe got the names of all the former tenants of the warehouse from the list he had developed. He called Pentell to discuss these tenants. Pentell called him back about 10 minutes later. Pentell described several of the tenants he remembered, but nothing worthwhile jumped out at Joe. Pentell also denied any knowledge of Paul Dalton, other than the radio, TV and newspaper coverage of his homicide, or any reason why Dalton would go to that warehouse.

Ginny then called Watkins, wanting to know whether Watkins or Aegis had ever had anything to do with that building. But Watkins had taken a day off and couldn't be reached. Ginny left a message for Watkins that Ginny would call her the next day.

Ginny then Googled the warehouse address. She came up with several items, most of which dealt with various tenants moving in and out over the years. There were also several items dealing with the blighted area of town in which that warehouse sat, and the need for the city or the state or someone to eventually do something about it. There were articles about the area having been considered and then no longer considered for a state prison to be built. Seeing these articles, Ginny recalled seeing this same news item a few times on TV. But Ginny didn't see anything that helped her figure out specifically why Dalton wound up in that warehouse.

Groping for straws, Ginny then began telephoning and checking with various city departments.

"Joe, got a min?"

"Sure. What up?"

"I'm running around in circles, or getting the run-around, or both."

"From who?"

"From our fair city. Watkins is unavailable until tomorrow. So I decided to check with the city. This is just a small city, but, I swear, it's as bureaucratic as the U.S. Army seems to be. I'm getting shuffled from the Building Department to Public Works to Economic Development to Housing & Property Management to who knows what."

"What specifically are you looking for?"

"That's part of the problem. I've got no idea. So I'm just asking them all whether they've had any dealings with that building or that part of town over the past few years."

"Yeah, I can see the problem. They don't know how to answer or research general questions. I bet the person answering the phone doesn't even know who to transfer you to."

"Got that right."

"You ought to go over to city hall and wander the building, asking the same questions, but in person, at the various departments. You'd have a better chance of bumping into some old fogy who knows something that can help us."

"Good suggestion. I'm on my way."

"Good luck. And, Ginny, when you're done, why don't you come over to my place? We can order in some pizza and have that 'us' discussion we started at lunch."

"Will do. What time?"

"Whenever. I was here real early this morning, so I'm bugging out soon."

"OK. See you later."

Chapter 26

"Ginny walked around the corner and entered the building through the front doors. Ginny almost always entered through the rear, as that was where the courts were. The building was an awkward amalgamation of old and new, much like the population of Jasper Creek, with the longtime farmers, factory workers and shopkeepers now intermingled with the newer, wealthier recent arrivals from the surrounding larger cities. The rear of the building, where the courtrooms, judges' offices, meeting rooms and holding cells were located, was a two-story, gray stone building built in the early 20th Century, with high ceilings, marble floors and large windows that could actually be opened and closed. About 15 years ago, a modern, all steel and glass, three-story addition had been attached to the front. The ground floor held the Chamber of Commerce and Tourist Information Center, a small cafe that served breakfast and lunch, and the receptionist for the city government. The second and third floors held the town council meeting room, several small meeting rooms and the various city government departments.

Ginny briefly reviewed the directory to the left of the two elevators, and then headed up the flight of stairs to the second floor. The first door on the right said "City Clerk." Ginny walked in and headed for the portly, middle-aged woman sitting behind the counter.

"Good afternoon. I'm Detective Harris. Can you help me?"

"Sure. What do you need?" said the woman as she struggled to stand up and face Ginny across the counter.

"We're investigating the recent homicide at 1220 Melrose Avenue."

"Oh, yes. I've seen that in the news. What a shame. What can I help you with?"

"Not sure. Just checking whether your office has had any recent dealings about that building or with any of its former tenants."

"Um. I can't think of anything we've dealt with regarding that building, but our office doesn't usually get involved with real estate issues. And I have no way of knowing who the former tenants were."

"Here's a list of the former tenants going back almost 20 years," said Ginny as she pulled the list out of her pocket-book and handed it to the clerk.

After a quick scan at the list, the clerk replied, "Nope."

"Nope what?"

"Nope. None of these names seem familiar," said the clerk as she handed the list back to Ginny.

"Which departments do you suggest I check with?"

"Depends."

"Depends on what?"

"On what you're looking for. There's the Assessor's and Tax Collector's offices if you're interested in property taxes. Or the Building Inspector if you're looking for code violations. Or Planning & Zoning if you want to do something else with that building. Or …."

"OK. I get it. My problem is that I don't have a specific

thing I'm trying to track down. Guess I'll just wander down the hall and try several departments."

"Yup. Good idea. And good luck."

"Thanks," said Ginny as she turned and walked back into the hall.

Ginny had similar unproductive visits to the Assessor's and then the Tax Collector's offices. The man in the Assessor's office and the lady in the Tax Collector's office were more talkative than the lady in the City Clerk's office, but neither had any useful information.

Getting increasingly frustrated, Ginny next entered the offices of the Planning & Zoning Commission.

"Hi, I'm Detective Harris. I'd like to speak with someone about the building at 1220 Melrose Avenue."

"Sure. Hold on a minute, detective. I'll see if Mr. Burton, our commissioner, is available."

"Thank you," said Ginny as the clerk disappeared into the rear offices.

A few minutes later, out came a tall, extremely thin man about 60 years old. His appearance, other than how thin he was, was unremarkable except for the long, gray handlebar moustache that curved around his mouth and seemed to extend halfway down to his shoulders.

"Hi, I'm Burt Burton. And, before you ask, yes, my parents did name me Burton."

"Pleased to meet you, sir. Thank you for seeing me so promptly."

"Glad to, especially since you and I have the same employer. What exactly can I help you with? Come on back to my palatial office suite."

Ginny walked around the counter and followed Burton

into his office. About 8 by 10 feet, with one small window, a metal desk and chair, two visitor chairs and a rusty gray filing cabinet, the office was a bit shy of being a palatial suite. Nonetheless, it was functional, with folders, drawings and other documents piled haphazardly on every horizontal surface except for Burton's chair and the two visitor chairs.

Burton sat behind his desk and Ginny sat in one of the visitor chairs.

"Mr. Burton, we're investigating the homicide that took place a month ago at 1220 Melrose Avenue. I'm checking to see if you or one of the other city departments might have had some involvement or issues with the property that might have a tie-in with my murder investigation."

"I don't even need to check the files on that building. I know all about it."

"Oh?"

"Those damn state bureaucrats in Columbus have been breaking our backsides over that building and the others on that street."

"How? What do you mean?"

"Don't you read the paper? This was big news in the Jasper Creek Gazette the past few months."

"I must admit, I'm not much of a newspaper reader. I catch CNN over breakfast most mornings, but that's about it. Fill me in, please."

"Well, as you know, that whole area of town has not been the high spot of Jasper Creek. Most of those buildings have been unoccupied for years. Unoccupied, that is, except for homeless folks, drug addicts, and teenagers out for a few thrills."

"Yes, I'm well aware of that. Our Patrol Division spends a disproportionate amount of its resources keeping the peace down there."

"I can only imagine. Well anyway, about a year ago, our friends in Columbus decided that they needed to build an additional prison. Knowing the problems they'd have with NIMBY, they split the process into two parts. Determine the type of prison needed, prepare the specs and get the funding approved as step one. Only after that was completed, begin the more politically sensitive task of deciding where to build it."

"Excuse me, but what's NIMBY? And I trust you will lead this discussion back to 1220 Melrose Avenue."

"NIMBY stands for 'Not In My Backyard.' This is a common phenomenon when dealing with projects like prisons or waste treatment facilities or subsidized housing. Even people, that is voters and political contributors, who support the project do not want it to be placed in their neighborhood, fearing increased crime or traffic, environmental issues and, ultimately, lower property values."

"And…"

"Hold on, detective. I'm getting to that now. Turns out that step one proceeded nicely. The need for a prison, specifically a minimum security prison, was agreed to and the state legislature appropriated funds for phase one, which would be the land acquisition and architectural design work."

"OK. And?"

"That's when the craziness started here. That blighted area, as well as two other areas elsewhere in the state, were selected as the best possible locations for the prison. You wouldn't believe the number of questions we started getting from the legislature, the architect and just about everyone else. We were working flat out just answering their questions and providing drawings and other stuff they requested. The Bureau of Prisons, oh, excuse me, the Department of Rehabilitation and Correction, to be politically correct, has been all over us."

"Yes, I'm aware of that. I saw enough TV and heard enough people talking to know that the area around that building was initially considered but was then eliminated as a possible site for the prison."

"That's correct. About six weeks ago, the formerly-known-as Bureau of Prisons and the architect concluded that to build the prison here, they'd have to knock down all the empty warehouses and build from scratch. The hope had been, and the preliminary budget had assumed, that most of the existing buildings could remain and just be remodeled. The cost estimate escalated so much that Jasper Creek was dropped as one of the possible locations."

"When exactly did all this take place?"

"Well, as I had said, the first step was accomplished about a year ago. The three prime locations were selected about six months ago, but they were only announced about four months ago. About two months after that they determined and announced that all the existing buildings here would have to be demolished to build the prison here. Then the decision to drop our location because of the price tag was made about six weeks ago.

"We've just about caught up on all our other work

now that they've stopped bombarding us with questions dealing with the prison project. You can probably check the old Jasper Creek and Columbus newspapers to get more details and exact dates."

"Yes, I'll do that. And thank you very much, Mr. Burton, for all your help."

"My pleasure. Hope it helps you catch the murderer."

"So do I," concluded Ginny as she exited Burton's office, the Planning & Zoning outer office and city hall.

Ginny wanted to race over to the library and search through the old Jasper Creek and Columbus newspapers to gather more details and exact dates. But, even more so, she wanted to race over to Joe's. Sure, she could hardly wait to bring him up to speed on her theory of why the vic was killed and left in that warehouse. But more important, she wanted to have that personal discussion with Joe. An easy decision — the library would still be there in the morning. Ginny walked back to her car, drove home, took a three-minute shower, dressed and was on her way to Joe's in record time.

Chapter 27

Joe answered the door. A bear hug, an extended kiss on the lips and Ginny was inside and the door closed.

"Hi, you look great. You even went home and changed."

"Yeah, I needed a quick shower after my tour of bureaucracy central. And now I need a drink."

"Beer or wine? Got both."

"Beer'd be fine."

Joe walked to the kitchen, took two beers out of the refrigerator and opened them. As Ginny had followed him into the small kitchen, he merely had to turn around from the counter to hand one of the bottles to her. "Here you go."

"Thanks. Nice and cold. Cheers."

"Cheers," repeated Joe as they clinked their bottles and each took a long, refreshing drink. "I was thinking of ordering in pizza. Work for you?"

"Sounds great. And if you have anything other than beer in the refrigerator, I can whip up a salad to go with it."

"Well, this is your lucky day. I stopped at the supermarket on the way home and loaded up on salad stuff, plus apple pie for dessert."

"Perfect. A typical Italian-American all-pie dinner. Pizza pie followed by apple pie."

While Joe called and ordered a large pizza, half with

various vegetables and half all meat, Ginny took the lettuce, tomato, cucumber, green pepper, scallions and radishes from the refrigerator, washed them and cut them into small pieces for a tossed salad.

"Ginny, want to start our discussion now or wait 'til later?"

"I want to fill you in about the warehouse. I think I got us a nice theory. Then let's have dinner, after which we can get into THE discussion."

"OK. Tell me about the warehouse."

"Well, after bouncing from department to department, I struck it rich with the Planning & Zoning commissioner. You were so right in telling me to deal with those agencies in person rather than by phone."

"OK. Good. Now get to the bottom line."

"Impatient, aren't we? The commissioner, Mr. Burton Burton if you can believe that, talked about how, before the killing, the state government had been looking at buying up the warehouse and some of the surrounding ones, knocking some of them completely down and building a minimum-security prison there. Shortly before the vic was killed, the state dropped Jasper Creek as one of the potential prison sites. And these plans and decisions were all over the Columbus and Jasper Creek newspapers and TV back then."

"Yeah, we knew all that. That's old news. Hell, we even talked about it a few times, how it would be great if that neighborhood got lifted out of the gutter."

"Yeah, but hearing about it in detail, lit up a lightbulb for me. The perp was either reminded or learned of these deserted warehouses by the news about the prison project. What could be a better place to kill a person and leave the body than a deserted warehouse in a deserted area of town, occupied only by a few homeless druggies? Heck, they'd probably be afraid to report it even if they found the body."

"Even better, if the perp was in Columbus, a dead body in Jasper Creek, especially if he were thought to be a homeless person, would get little or no notice in Columbus."

"You bet. Tomorrow morning I'm going to the library to check the old newspapers to see exactly what was said exactly when."

"Good idea. But I think you've figured out why the vic was killed in that warehouse."

"Yes, so do I. Now we have to figure out who, and how he or she tricked or forced him to go to that warehouse."

"Yup. But we're a big step ahead of where we were before. Well done."

"Thanks. But there was a hunk of luck involved."

"Doesn't matter. We don't get a pass when we hit bad luck, so our successes shouldn't be reduced when we get some good luck."

"Fair enough. How about another beer while we wait for the pizza?"

"Coming right up."

The pizza was delivered about 10 minutes later. Joe and Ginny devoured it, along with the salad and another beer for each of them. Wrapping up with coffee and large slices of the apple pie that had been warming in the oven, Joe and Ginny both felt stuffed. With no pots and pans, the cleanup was completed in short order.

"OK, Joe. Grab another beer if you want. I'm fine without one. Let's go sit in the living room and discuss."

"Coming. Just let me grab my brew."

Joe and Ginny were sitting in the living room, Ginny at the end of the couch and Joe in the easy chair placed next to it at a 90-degree angle. Joe felt like he used to when he would get called to the high school principal's office.

"Ginny, I gotta tell you. I really want to have this discussion, but I'm scared shitless."

"You're not the only one. But we need to do this."

"I know. How do we start? I'm not the greatest at talking about stuff like this."

"I know you're not, Joe. How about I start, just by jumping in and rambling through my thoughts. And then it'll be your turn."

"OK. Go for it."

Ginny sat there for a few minutes, trying to figure out how to begin.

"OK. Here goes. Joe, you know that I was married for a few years right after high school, but the marriage fell apart once I became a cop."

"Yeah, I know that."

"He was a good guy, but he couldn't handle my being a cop. It made him feel like I was tougher and more manly than he was."

"Well, you are pretty tough, but I'd never describe you as manly."

"Anyway, it was a friendly split, he moved away and that was that. I thought I got over it pretty quick, but it clearly had a bigger impact on me than I thought."

"How so?"

"I never consciously decided it, but I never had a serious, or even half-serious, relationship after that. Until now. I can't even tell you why. Probably some combination of fear of getting dumped again and losing respect for all men."

"Wow. That's pretty broad, blaming all men."

"I know. I didn't even realize I was feeling that way until you and I started getting so close, and … well, you know. And now I'm loving being with you, but worried that I'm somehow going to get dumped again. I had pretty much made up my mind that I was destined to be single and alone forever. Sure, I have friends, even a few male ones, but you're still sort of alone with just friends."

"I know what you mean."

"And I'm really scared. If we break up at some point, not only will I be hurt badly, but I'm afraid that I'll also lose my best friend. Joe, I'm telling you this, but I don't really know why. There's nothing we can do about it. Even if you promise to never leave me, like they do in the movies, we have no idea what will happen. You can't promise to control your future thoughts and feelings."

Joe leaned over and took Ginny's left hand in both of his. They both sat there for a few minutes, each deep in their own thoughts.

"Ginny, it seems like you made my speech for me. And you said it better than I could. Just replace your divorce with that damn drunk killing Lori and Adam and it's my story. And on top of all that, as much as being with you is fantastic, I wind up feeling guilty, like I'm cheating on Lori."

"Oh, Joe."

"I know it's stupid, but I can't help it."

"I never met Lori, but I feel like I sort of know her from all you've said about her over the years. And I bet she wouldn't think you're cheating on her. She'd want you to get on with your life and be happy. She'd be upset if she felt she was holding you back."

"I know that. It's just something that I feel, even though it's irrational. Luckily, it's getting weaker as time goes on."

"Well, that's good. Joe, if you ever feel that I'm pushing you or us too fast, you have to let me know."

"Will do."

"OK, all those beers and coffee are doing a number on me. Time out for a trip to the little girl's room. When I get back, let's move the discussion to item number 2."

"Item number 2? What's that?"

"Where's this heading? Where do we want it to go? Will we manage it or just let it find its own course? And, finally, what, if anything, do we do about the chief and the department?"

"Wow. This could be a late night. Go do your thing. I'm right behind you after you're done."

Five minutes later, Joe and Ginny were back in their same seats in the living room.

"OK, Joe, where do you think this is going? And where do you want it to go?"

"That's a tough question. The first part, I mean. In theory, this could go just about any place, from breaking up next week to getting married and living happily ever after. Or any point in between."

"Joe, you just gave me the theoretical answer of everything possible. Now tell me where you think this is going, not every place that it could theoretically go."

"Ginny, I've asked myself that same damn question dozens of times. I know where I'd like it to go, but I'm less than sure of it going that way."

"OK. Where would you like it to go?"

"I feel like I've come alive again since we started our relationship, or whatever we should call it. I mean being your partner and friend is great, but this is different. I'm not sure about marriage, at least not yet, but I feel like I'd like to spend the rest of my life with you."

"Oh, Joe," said Ginny as she got up from the couch, straddled Joe's legs and gave him a deep, long kiss.

"I assume that means that you don't disagree."

"Yup. You're one hell of a good detective. But, seriously, Joe, I do feel the same. Marriage may or may not be in the picture at some point, but being together with you is something I really want."

"Ginny, do you think we're moving too fast?"

"No, unless it feels too fast for you. Don't forget, we've been partners for four years, spending more waking hours together than most married people. Even when we don't have to, like most lunchtimes, we voluntarily choose to be together."

"You're right. And if we're not sick of each other by now, there's a good chance we'll never get sick of each other."

"I sure hope that's the case."

"Me too."

"OK. Now, Joe, what do we do about the chief and the department?"

"I say nothing for now. I'm sure there's a department policy, or the chief will write one, about partners not dating each other, much less living together or being married."

"We should find out if there is a policy, and what it says."

"Fair enough. But that won't happen tonight. How about we crawl into bed and let nature take its course. Tomorrow's another day."

"Works for me."

And 10 minutes later, Joe turned off the last remaining light and climbed into bed with Ginny. And, sure enough, nature took its course.

Chapter 28

As it had been set to do, the alarm rang at 7 sharp. Joe moaned, rolled over, hit the snooze button and rolled back to the cuddling position in which he and Ginny had been sleeping.

"OK, Ginny, I've arranged for the alarm clock to give us a 10-minute reprieve."

"Great. If you can do that 10 more times, I'll be ready to get up."

"Sorry. But no further extensions. As you know, the early bird gets the worm."

"What the hell do you think I want a worm for?"

"Nonetheless, we do have to get up and get to work."

"I know. And, Joe, thanks for the discussion last night. I understand how you don't like that sort of thing, but I think we needed to have that talk."

"I agree. I'm glad we did, even though I wasn't too excited beforehand."

"Yeah, at least we clarified a few things. We both feel the same about each other, which is the most important thing. And we both have similar fears and concerns. And we'll keep our relationship or situation or whatever it's called quiet for now, at least until we find out about the chief and the department's policies."

"Well summarized. Now, time to get up. Let's see if we can both squeeze into the shower at the same time."

Thirty minutes later, dressed and having had an orange

juice, toast and coffee breakfast, they were off to work, Joe to the PD and Ginny to the library.

While sitting in her car waiting for the Jasper Creek library to open at 9:30, Ginny called Watkins' office.

"Good morning, Aegis Control Corporation. How may I direct your call?"

"This is Detective Harris. I'd like to speak with Captain Watkins."

"Yes, detective. One minute please. Captain Watkins said she was expecting your call and I should put you right through."

"Great. Thanks."

"Hello, detective. This is Captain Watkins. I was told that you called yesterday and said you'd be calling back today. Sorry I wasn't available yesterday. How can I help you today?"

"Captain, I want to ask you about a building in Jasper Creek."

"What? We've already been through that. Yes, I helped our Security Consulting subsidiary lease that office spa …"

"Hold on, Captain. That's not the building I'm calling about. Have you, or Aegis Control, or Security Consulting or any other entity or person you know or deal with had anything to do with an empty warehouse at 1220 Melrose Avenue in Jasper Creek?"

"The answer is yes. Ted, Mr. Pentell that is, told me about the murder victim found there. And I know that Mr. Pentell's company owns that building. And knowing about Mr. Dalton's murder, all your questions lead me to assume that he's the victim in Ted's building."

"Anything else?"

"No. That's all I know about it. And neither I nor any part of Aegis ever had anything to do with that building. I don't think I've ever even seen it, unless I drove by at some point without knowing it."

"OK. Thanks for answering my questions. Have a nice day."

"That's it? Nothing else?"

"Yes, that's it for now. We'll be in touch if anything else comes up. Good-bye."

"Uh, yes, good-bye."

By now the library had opened. Ginny got out of her car and walked in, heading directly for the librarian's counter along the left wall.

"Good morning, ma'am. How can I help you?"

"I'd like you to show me where the microfiche, or whatever technology's now used, of old newspapers from Jasper Creek and Columbus are. And I'll need you to show me how to use the machine."

"Sure, I'd be happy to. Please follow me," said the librarian as she came from behind the counter and walked to the rear wall of the room."

"What dates are you looking for? We have them going back more than 40 years."

"This ought to be fairly easy then. I'm looking for the papers going back just a couple of months."

"Oh, why didn't you say so? Papers that recent are actually physically stored here in the library. We only get digital versions of the papers after about a year. Follow me. Here you go. This stack is the Jasper Creek Gazette and this is the Columbus Dispatch. The most current issues are here and the older ones are on the lower shelves."

"OK. Thanks."

"Just two other things, if you don't mind. First, it's fine to take papers out of the pile, but, please, please, please put them back in the right pile in the correct chronological order."

"Will do. And the other thing?"

"If you will want to be making copies, that large printer over there can copy a whole newspaper page at once. The price is 15 cents per copy. Come back to my desk and I'll give you a code to use. The code lets you operate the copier and also keeps track of the number of copies you make so we know how much to charge you."

"Great. Let's get started."

Ginny followed her back to the counter, got her 4-digit copier code and was soon sitting at a table opposite the piles of newspapers. Ginny began with the Jasper Creek papers, starting with eight weeks before the homicide.

Ginny was surprised at how long this effort was going to take. She had to carefully scan every page of every day's paper. It's not like there was an index to direct her to the right editions and pages. And the Columbus papers were more than twice as thick as the Jasper Creek ones.

After a half-hour, Ginny stepped into the hallway and called Joe.

"Hi, Joe. Doing anything useful?"

"Always. In fact I got an e-mail from Bill, my old Army buddy, saying he'll be calling me in about 15 minutes. How're you doing?"

"I'm here in the library, buried up to my you-know-what in newspapers. This is going to take forever. After your call, how'd you like to join me? We could get done twice as fast."

"Sure. I'd love to be buried in your you-know-what. I'll be there in about 45 minutes."

"Joe, you're an angel. I appreciate it."

"That's what partners are for."

"You'll find me sprawled out at a table in the back of the main room. And, to show you my appreciation, I'll buy lunch."

"Now I'm definitely coming over. See you soon."

"Thanks, Joe," said Ginny as she hung up and returned to her stacks of newspapers.

Chapter 29

Right on schedule, Joe's phone rang 15 minutes later.

"Hello. Detective McFarland."

"Well, what an amazing coincidence. I was trying to call a Detective McFarland."

"Hiya, Bill. Thanks for calling. Whadda ya have for me?"

"Afraid not much at all. I did confirm all the assignments and dates you gave me. But that's about it. There were serious rumors and allegations about stolen stuff from Pentell's operation in Germany, but nothing was ever proved and they didn't go forward with any charges. As for some of the other characters, despite my working at the Pentagon, I couldn't get any more info about special ops than you did. When they say secretive, they mean secretive."

"Well, I appreciate your efforts, Bill. At least you were able to confirm the few facts we do have."

"Yeah, sorry I couldn't help more."

"No sweat. And, Bill, we do need to get together for dinner one of these days."

"I'm going to hold you to that, buddy. Good luck with your investigation. And take care."

"You, too. Bye."

Disappointed but not surprised, Joe made a few notes

about the call while it was still fresh in his mind, and then headed to the library to give Ginny a hand.

Joe quietly walked up behind Ginny and asked. "Is there a you-know-what buried under all those papers?"

Smiling to herself, Ginny responded. "You'll have to start digging and find out for yourself. Seriously, Joe, thanks for coming. I'm about halfway through the Jasper Creek papers. I found a few good articles and copied them. Why don't you start with the Columbus papers? Here, let me show you how and where the papers are stacked and how to use the copier when you find something. I started with papers going back eight weeks before the homicide. And, most important, the librarian warned that it's a capital offense if we don't return the newspapers to their right piles in the right chronological order."

"Got it. I'm ready to go."

Almost three hours later, Ginny and Joe had gone through all the papers and had photocopied about 20 articles.

"OK, Ginny, let's take these copies and grab some lunch. Besides starving to death, I can't wait to see you pay for my lunch."

"Roger that. Just let me go thank the librarian and pay for the copies we made."

And a few minutes later, "Tacos, I assume?"

"For a change, let's walk over to Krogers. They have tables where you can sit and eat."

"That's fine with me. But quite revolutionary for you."

Once inside Kroger, Ginny picked up a large soda from the refrigerated section and ordered a ham, turkey and cheese sandwich on Italian bread, to which she added a small bag of potato chips. Joe went to the salad bar, made a heaping salad of all types of vegetables and topped it with a balsamic vinaigrette dressing. He also grabbed a diet soda. Ginny paid for it all and they both walked over to an empty table and sat down.

"Why the rabbit food, Joe? You sick or something?"

"No, I'm on a serious diet now."

"What? Since when? You haven't dieted, or even slightly watched what you eat, since I met you."

"I know. Seems out of character, doesn't it?"

"Totally. When did you start the diet?"

"About two hours ago."

"What?"

"No, really. I've been thinking about it, and finally decided to bite the bullet."

"Why, Joe? You're not heavy. You don't need to lose weight."

"Yes and no. I actually weigh the same, within a couple of pounds of what I did 10 years ago."

"See?"

"But more of the weight is now belly fat rather than muscle. I want to lose this gut that's starting to grow."

"Joe, you don't have a big gut. I may be biased, but I think you look great. Why did this come up now?"

"Thanks for the compliment, but I do need to knock off 5 or 10 pounds."

"And why now?"

"Um, well, you."

"Huh?"

"After our discussion last night about us, I decided to get back into shape."

"Oh, Joe. I'm flattered, but you really don't have to do this for me. I'm perfectly happy with you just the way you are."

"Well, thanks. But I'm not."

"OK, then. Go for it. And I'll support you anyway I can."

"Thanks, partner."

"And when you finish your rabbit food and I finish this yummy, oops, I mean horrible tasting and disgusting sandwich, let's head back and see what we can make of all the newspaper article copies we made."

"Sounds like a plan," said Joe as he chomped down on another piece of iceberg lettuce.

Chapter 30

Back at PD headquarters, Joe and Ginny laid out on the conference room table all the newspaper copies they had made at the library. Splitting the papers into two piles, one for the Jasper Creek Gazette and the other for the Columbus Dispatch, they then put each pile into chronological order, with the oldest one on top.

"OK," said Ginny as she walked to the whiteboard and picked up a black marker. "Let's start with the Columbus papers. Read me each date and give me a summary of the article. I'll try to write the info on the board."

"Will do. Here we go. This article is from the June 12th paper. Let's see. It talks about how the state prison commission is meeting to review the three potential sites selected for the prison."

Ginny wrote the date and brief summary of the article on the whiteboard. "OK, Joe, what's the next article?"

Joe and Ginny continued this for the next hour and a half, taking only one short break for the bathrooms and a coffee refill. When finished, Ginny had just about the entire whiteboard covered with newspaper dates and article summaries, the left side of the board for the Columbus paper and the right side for the Jasper Creek paper.

"Ginny, I think we got something. Your trip to the

library was a great idea. It's clear that anyone reading either of these papers from mid-June up until the time of the murder would know that the warehouse and its neighboring buildings had been on a shortlist of locations for the new prison, but then was dropped as an option. There was a lot of newspaper coverage about that area of town, how empty and desolate it is with only some homeless and druggies in the area. That would make the warehouse a pretty nice location for a murder."

"It sure would. And even if the murderer didn't read newspapers, I'm sure this info was all over the Columbus and Jasper Creek TV and radio stations."

"No doubt about it."

"It's interesting. We, of course, knew about the whole prison thing from the get-go. But how all this publicity probably gave the murderer the idea to commit the murder here didn't register with us until our visits to city hall and the library."

"Well done, partner. Ginny, I think you've answered the question about why this location for the murder. Now we still need to figure out who did it and why they did it, and how he or she got Dalton to that warehouse."

"Yup. And I'll betcha 10 bucks that we'll answer those questions if we can figure out who the mysterious Sergeant Andrews is. I know one thing. Ghosts don't leave voicemail messages on people's cell phones."

"Yeah, you're probably right. Most ghosts prefer to text rather than call."

"Joe, I'm glad you're so up to date on your ghostology, or whatever it's called."

"Well, in any event, what say you get that stuff on the board typed into your computer and then we call it a day?"

"Boy, you're just full of great ideas today. Give me about 20 minutes or so and then I'll be ready."

"No need for me to wait for you. We need to travel in separate cars anyhow. I'll swing by the store and get some dinner. I'll park in the street and leave the garage open so you can sneak your car right in there."

"OK, see you later."

"You bet."

Ninety minutes later, Joe and Ginny were sitting in Joe's kitchen, finishing the lo mein and the rest of the white rice.

"This was a nice change, Joe. Thanks for thinking of Chinese."

"Yeah, it's been a while since I've had it. And the best part, like with pizza, there're no dishes or pots to wash. Just dump everything in the garbage."

"That is nice. Here, let me give you a hand."

"Hang on, we're not quite finished with dinner yet."

"Huh? The boxes are empty. And so is the wine bottle. What's left?

"Dessert."

"Dessert? You never get dessert with Chinese food."

"Sure you do. Hold on." Joe got up and reached into the shopping bag on the counter and returned to the table with two fortune cookies in his hand."

"Oh, fortune cookies. Of course. How could I have forgotten?"

Joe held out his hand and opened his fingers. "Pick one."

"OK," said Ginny as she picked one of the fortune cookies. "Joe, these are all cracked and broken. It looks like they were destroyed and then some amateur tried to reassemble them."

"Yeah, I must have had them at the bottom of the bag with the food on top of them. Sorry. Anyhow, most people don't even eat them. They just want to see what their fortune is. Go ahead. What does your fortune say?"

"OK, here goes," said Ginny as she further broke her fortune cookie and took out the small piece of folded paper.

"Well? Read it."

Ginny unfolded the paper and then exclaimed, "Somebody loves me!"

"We know that. But what does your fortune say?"

"That is what it says. Somebody loves me."

"Wow. These fortunes are more accurate than I thought."

"What does yours say, Joe."

"Oh, nothing special. It doesn't matter."

"Yes it does," said Ginny as she grabbed the other fortune cookie from Joe, took out the piece of paper and unfolded it. "It says the same thing as mine. Hey, wait a minute."

"What?"

"Joe, that's the sweetest thing. You broke open both fortune cookies and replaced the original fortunes with these."

"OK, I confess. I wanted to be sure that the fortune

cookie you chose was true. So I typed two copies of this replacement fortune. I had to do it with both cookies 'cause I couldn't know which one you'd pick. Sorry I didn't have time to include some Chinese symbols on the little pieces of paper."

"Joe, is this your way of saying that you ..."

"Yes, it is. And it's true."

"Well, guess what? Your fortune is also true. I can vouch for it."

"Ginny, I think we just took another big step in our relationship."

"Yes, sir. We did. And perhaps now we should cele-brate."

Needless to say, the empty Chinese food containers and chopsticks weren't thrown away until the next morning.

Chapter 31

Joe and Ginny arrived at PD HQ early the next morning, each in their own car. They were at the chief's door as soon as he arrived, just after 8 o'clock.

"Morning, Chief," said Ginny. "Got a minute for Joe and me to fill you in on the progress we made yesterday on the warehouse homicide?"

"Sure do. I can always make time to hear good news. Come on in."

Joe and Ginny entered the chief's office and stood in front of his desk.

"Go ahead, Joe. Give him the news."

"No way, Ginny. The progress resulted from your efforts, so you tell him."

"OK, but it was a team effort. Chief, we're pretty sure we know why that warehouse was chosen as the kill site."

"Great. Spit it out. I'm anxious to hear why."

"Well, as you know, that warehouse and several others nearby were being considered by the state as a great location for a new prison."

"Yes, I've been aware of that. I also know that the state recently dropped that area as one of the possible options."

"That's true," said Ginny. "We checked the Jasper Creek and Columbus newspapers for the two months before the murder. This whole prison project, possibly on and then off, got a lot of press. The articles also were very descriptive of how desolate that part of town is. We think the perp, either reading the paper or watching TV, became aware of or was reminded of this area and what an attractive place it would be for a murder. And for leaving the body. There was a good chance that the body wouldn't be found for quite a while, and when it was, it would be largely ignored as just another homeless or druggie killing. Hell, it might not even make the Columbus news."

"Sounds plausible to me. Funny how often the simple explanation turns out to be the right one. Have you figured out how the murderer got the victim to go there from Columbus? And, more important, who the murderer is?"

"No, not yet," interjected Joe. "But we're working on it."

"But it does sound like you're pretty well convinced that it was premeditated murder. We can skip self-defense or accidental."

"That's right, Chief. We think the perp got the vic there somehow, and not to go sightseeing," said Joe.

"Good. Thanks for the update. Now why don't you two get back to work?"

"We're on our way, Chief," said Ginny as she and Joe left the chief's office and settled in at their own desks.

"Hey, Joe, there's a message here for me to call the medical examiner back. I'm gonna call him now. Ginny dialed the number and put her phone on speaker.

"Jasper Creek Medical Examiner's Office. This is Dr. Baxton. How may I help you?"

"Hi, Doc. This is Ginny Harris. I have a message to call you guys."

"Oh, hi, Ginny. Yes, I left that message a few minutes ago. We've completed our work on the body of Paul

Dalton, the victim in that warehouse shooting last month. We've eked out every possible piece of information from the body."

"That's good. Any new findings to report?"

"No. Just further confirmation of what we already knew. The reason I called was to let you know it's now OK to ship the body back to his home. We've got no further need for it."

"Thanks for calling. I'll get this info to our contact with the Kansas City police. He'll talk to the victim's widow. She had said that she'll pay for and arrange shipping the body home."

"Good. You can give her my name and phone number to work out the details on this end."

"Will do. Thanks, Doc."

"Don't mention it. See ya."

"Bye."

"Well, Joe. I'll call Sergeant James and have him contact Dalton's widow."

"I'm sure she'll be less than thrilled to have to handle all this. And pay for it. He didn't treat her exactly first class before he died."

"Very true. But we can't guess how she might feel toward the vic regardless of all that."

"I agree. In fact, it's pretty tough to guess how anyone feels about anything."

Ginny called Sergeant James in Kansas City and got right through to him. After she explained the reason for her call, he said that he would drive out and talk with Mrs. Dalton, after which he'd call Ginny back. Ginny thanked him and hung up.

Early that afternoon, Sergeant James called Ginny back. "Hello, detective, this is Sergeant James in Kansas City."

"Hi. Sergeant. Thanks for calling me back."

"I met with the widow. She was all non-emotional business. It was like we were talking about a distant relative rather than her husband, even if they were separated."

"And?"

"She readily agreed, as she had earlier, to arrange for the body's transportation and funeral and to pay for them. She said that her husband had always said he wanted to be cremated and that's what she'd arranged. She repeatedly emphasized that cremation was because that's what her husband wanted, not because it's cheaper than a burial."

"Well, in any event, her taking care of this makes our lives simpler."

"Yes, it does. She said that she'll have the funeral home they'll be using call your medical examiner and they can work out the details among themselves."

"Makes sense."

"And by the way, I and Patrolman Jakowski will attend the funeral once it's scheduled. We'll represent the KC PD as well as you folks in Ohio."

"Very thoughtful. I'm sure the widow will appreciate the gesture."

"Yes. I also make it a practice to attend funerals of murder victims, just in case we can learn something by who else is attending and how they're acting."

"Very smart. Thanks for everything. I'm sure we'll be in touch."

"Yes, so am I. Bye."

Ginny next called Captain Watkins and informed her of the plans to return the body to Kansas City. Ginny asked Watkins to pass that information on to Alan Meyers in Afghanistan as Ginny and Joe had agreed to keep him up to date with developments in the case. Watkins said that she would.

Joe and Ginny soon left work. They again spent almost the entire weekend inside Joe's house, other than for a few drives in the countryside. They spent less time having sex and more time talking with each other and getting to know each other in a more in-depth and meaningful way than they had in all of the past few years working together.

Chapter 32

Monday morning found Joe and Ginny back at their desks, with their ever-handy cups filled with fresh coffee.

"Ok, Joe, let's plan out our next moves."

"Yeah, let's do it before the chief asks us what our plans are. For some odd reason, he's rarely satisfied whenever I tell him that our plan is to develop a plan."

"Wonder why he's so unreasonable? But, seriously, now that we know why the vic was in that warehouse, we need to determine what and who brought him there."

"Can't argue with that."

"Let's listen once again to that voicemail message from the mysterious, or non-existent, Sergeant Andrews. And then we should play it for each of our cast of characters to see if they recognize the voice or any background noise."

"Good idea, Ginny. We ought to start with the good colonel and his trusty sidekick, Tonto. Oh, I mean Watkins. And also Watkins' sidekick, Pentell."

"Right. And if we strike out, we should then widen the audience. We can try the vic's wife, or rather widow, his buddy Meyers and even Meyers' mother."

"OK. Enough of this heavy-duty planning. Let's get to it."

Joe went to the evidence room and brought back the recorded copy of the voicemail message that had been left on Dalton's cell phone. He and Ginny listened to the message three times, but did not recognize the voice or hear, much less recognize, any distinct background sounds.

They then called Watkins, followed by Burke, and explained what they were doing and then played the tape. In fact, at his request, they played it a second time for Burke. But both strongly confirmed that they still didn't recognize the voice or any background sounds.

"Well, that's strike two," said Joe. "Since he's so nearby, let's walk over to Pentell's office and do this in person."

"Sure. I'd love a pleasant little morning stroll," said Ginny with a smile.

A few minutes later, they were in Pentell's reception area. After a brief wait while he finished a phone call, he came out and led them back into his office.

"Good morning, detectives. What can I do for you?"

"Mr. Pentell, we have here a copy of the voicemail message that was left on the murder victim's cell phone. We believe this was the first step in somehow getting him to go to your empty warehouse. We'd like you to listen to it carefully a couple of times. Let us know if you recognize the voice or if you recognize any background noises."

"OK. I'll give it a shot."

After listening to the tape twice, Pentell shook his head. "Sorry, but I don't recognize the voice and I didn't even hear any background noises."

"Well, thanks for trying," said Ginny. "One other thing. How come you never mentioned to us the possibility of the state taking over your building and several adjacent ones to build a prison?"

"I only wish. First of all, I didn't mention it because I

never thought it was relevant to the recent murder. And secondly, that prison is only the latest rumor of several over the past few years of the state going to take it over for a prison, or warehouses, or an office complex. There have also been rumors of the city taking it for a road repair or a snow plowing facility. But these never seem to pan out for one reason or another. And, in case you haven't heard yet, the prison possibility has recently been killed for cost reasons. So I'm still stuck with this big, empty building, wanted by no one, and costing me ongoing money for insurance and maintenance and property taxes."

"Understood," said Joe. "Well, good luck to you with the building. And please be sure to contact us if you think of anything that might be useful to our case."

"Thank you. And I will, of course. Good-bye for now."

"Good-bye, Mr. Pentell," said Joe and Ginny in unison.

Although only about 11 o'clock, Joe and Ginny went around the corner from PD headquarters for an early lunch at Sancho's. True to form, two burritos for Joe and one for Ginny, with large Diet Cokes for both.

"Well, Joe. I see you've completed your diet. Was that one lunch of just having a salad that effective?"

"Yup, it sure was. It was extremely difficult for me, but I managed for the entire meal. And now that I'm back to my trim, fighting form, I can return to normal eating."

"Joe, I applaud all the self-control you had during your one-meal diet. And the great results you've achieved. But, regardless, don't ever try to describe your regular eating pattern as 'normal.' I see what you usually eat, and it isn't normal."

"OK, OK. Gimme a break."

"Will do. And, besides, I told you that I thought your bod was just fine and you didn't need to diet."

"Yes you did. And I appreciate that."

Back at their desks, Joe and Ginny decided to try the voicemail message tape with what they had called the wider cast of characters.

"Joe, we can do this by phone with Dalton's widow and Meyer's mother, but I don't think the voice quality of the call with Meyers in Afghanistan is anywhere good enough for him to have a shot at recognizing anything."

"You're right. Let's check with Watkins. Maybe they have some kind of higher quality system that we can use."

"Good idea. I'll give her a call right now. After that, we can try to get hold of the vic's widow and Meyers' mother."

Ginny rummaged through her desk drawer and pulled out Watkins' phone number and called her. "Hello, Captain Watkins. This is Detective Harris from Jasper Creek."

"Good afternoon, detective. How can I help you this time?"

"Captain, we'd like to play the taped voicemail message we have for Alan Meyers to see if he recognizes anyone or anything. Just like we did with you and the colonel. But we think the audio quality of the video phone call we had with him is not high enough to give him a good chance of recognizing anything. Does Aegis have any systems with higher-quality audio?"

"You're definitely right, detective. That audio quality can be pretty bad. Fortunately, we do have a higher-quality system, but it's voice only. No video."

"That would be fine. We don't need video for this. How quickly could you set such a call up?"

"Well, not for the next several days."

"Oh, that's disappointing. Isn't there some way you could arrange this sooner?"

"Oh, I'm sorry. I guess you hadn't heard. Mr. Meyers requested time off so that he could return to Missouri to attend Mr. Dalton's funeral. In fact, he's probably within an hour or two of departing Afghanistan now. We obviously granted his request. He's not immediate family, so his time off will be without pay. Fortunately for him, he was able to grab a free ride on one of our planes heading back to the States now. That'll take him into Dulles in Washington, and from there he presumably booked his own flight to Missouri."

"No, we hadn't heard that. How long will he be in the U.S.?"

"We granted him one week of leave. So excluding travel days, if he takes the whole week, he'll basically be in the U.S. for five days."

"Great. That'll make our job a lot easier. Could you please get a message to him to contact us as soon as he can?"

"Sure. I'll be happy to. Depending on his layover in D.C., I assume he'll either call you from there or from Kansas City when he arrives."

"That would be fine. Thanks for your help. Bye for now."

"You're very welcome. Good-bye."

Chapter 33

"Hello."

"Hello, Ms. Dalton. This is Detectives Harris and McFarland calling from Ohio."

"Oh, hello. Does this mean you have some news for me?"

"Not yet. But we are making progress. In fact, we have a recording of a voicemail message from your husband's phone. We'd like to play it for you to see if you recognize the voice or perhaps any special background noises."

"OK, I'd be happy to try. Just let me put my daughter in the other room so it's quieter here. Hold on a minute."

A couple of minutes later, "OK, I'm back. Go ahead and play the message."

Ginny played the message, but the widow didn't recognize the voice or any sounds. "Sorry, detectives, but I don't think I can be of any help."

"Well, thank you for trying, Ms. Dalton. We heard that the medical examiner has released your husband's body. Is everything working out with you getting the body back home?"

"Oh, yes. Thank you for asking. Everyone has been so helpful. The funeral home expects to have Paul — er, the body — back here on Wednesday, and the funeral is scheduled for Friday morning."

"Wow. That's efficient."

"Yeah, we had to. Alan Meyers is flying back from Afghanistan for the funeral and he only has a few days off. And Paul would be devastated if Alan couldn't be at the funeral."

"We understand. Well, thank you for all your help. And again, our sincere sympathies."

"Thank you. And you will let me know when you learn more? I really want the S.O.B. who did this to pay for it."

"Yes, we'll keep you informed. Bye for now."

"Good-bye."

"Those two guys must have been really good buddies for Meyers to come back from Afghanistan for the funeral."

"Yeah, as we were told, they were best friends going all the way back to grade school. At any rate, we'll be able to play that message for him when he calls us once he's in the U.S."

"That's true, Joe. In the meantime, it's probably a long shot, but let me get Meyers' mother's phone number so we can play the tape for her."

"OK."

Ginny's phone rang while she was searching for the phone number. "Hello. Detective Harris."

"Hello, detective. This is Sergeant James from Kansas City. Just calling to make sure you're up to date. The body apparently is about ready to be shipped back here, and the funeral is scheduled for this Friday at 10 a.m. There won't be any cemetery burial as the body will be cremated."

"Hi, Sergeant. Thanks for keeping us in the loop. Still planning on attending the funeral?"

"Yes, Officer Jakowski and I will be there. We'll let you know if we see anything worth noting."

"Great. We appreciate all your help. Take care."

"Same to you. Stay safe."

Ginny found the phone number and called Mrs. Meyers. She listened to the tape, but didn't recognize anyone or anything.

"Thank you for trying to help, Mrs. Meyers."

"You're welcome. I just wish I could have been more help."

"You tried. That's all we can ask. Will you be going to Mr. Dalton's funeral?"

"Yes, of course. He and Alan were so close, he was almost a second son for me."

"Despite the sad reason," said Ginny, "I'm sure you'll be glad to see your son."

"What? What do you mean?"

"Oh, I'm sorry, Mrs. Meyers. I assumed you knew. Your son is flying home for the funeral."

"Oh, my goodness. I had no idea. I bet he was planning on surprising me. Don't worry. I'll act surprised when I see him or if he calls to tell me. He won't know that you spoiled the surprise."

"Uh, yes. Thank you. Well, good-bye for now. And thanks for trying to help."

"You're welcome. Good-bye."

Chapter 34

The next morning around 11, Joe's phone rang. "Good morning. Detective McFarland here."

"Good morning, detective. This is Alan Meyers. Captain Watkins said you wanted me to call as soon as I arrived in the U.S. Sorry I couldn't call you from Washington, but I had a tight connection for the flight to KC."

"Not a problem, Mr. Meyers. Thanks for calling. Hold on a second. Let me put you on the speaker. Detective Harris is here with me."

"Good morning, Mr. Meyers."

"Hello, detective. Yeah, I guess it is morning. Someplace. I've been traveling for just under 24 hours so I have no idea what day it is, much less the time."

"We understand," said Ginny. "Where are you now?"

"At Kristi's, Paul's widow."

"Oh," said Ginny.

"Yeah, I came here right from the airport. Poor Kristi. She's all alone at this emotional time. And this is after all that Paul put her through these past few years. She needs someone to support her now. Her parents are in the area, but that's not the same thing, if you know what I mean."

"You must be a good friend, Mr. Meyers. I'm sure that Ms. Dalton appreciates having you there."

"There's no way I wouldn't be here."

"By the way," added Ginny. "We spoke with your

mother yesterday, and she didn't know you were going to be there."

"Yeah, things happened so fast, I haven't yet had a chance to call her. Now that I'm here, I will of course."

"Mr. Meyers, the reason we wanted to speak with you is that we have a recording of a voicemail message that was left on Mr. Dalton's cell phone shortly before he was killed. We'd like you to listen to it to see if you recognize the voice. Or any of the background sounds."

"Sure. Anything to help. Now?"

"Yes, now would be great if you have the time."

"Sure. Now is fine. Just one minute. Hey, Kristi, I'll be with you in a few minutes, as soon as this phone call is over. OK, detectives, I'm ready."

Ginny played the tape twice for Meyers.

"Mr. Meyers, did you recognize the voice or any of the background sounds?"

"Umm, I'm not sure. Could you play that message one more time for me?"

"Sure," said Ginny as she replayed the message again. "Do you recognize the voice? Or any background sounds?"

"No. Sorry. I thought I did, but no, I don't."

"Are you sure?" asked Joe.

"Yes. Positive. But that message sure explains why Paul was so mysterious about having to postpone his visit to Aegis. Do you think the person on that recording is the one who killed Paul?"

"We don't know yet. But that's why we're trying to identify him. He may be the murderer. Or he may be an accomplice. We just don't know yet," answered Joe.

"Well, I sure hope you find the damn murderer. It's still unbelievable that Paul's dead. And poor Krisi here all alone. I'll try to spend as much time as I can with her over the next few days, but then I have to head back overseas. I do get one-month of leave, but only after six months. That's a long time to wait. I don't know how she's going to make it. Alone and with a three-year-old child. I mean she's got her parents for some help, but, like I said, that's not the same thing."

"Mr. Meyers, when are you leaving to return to the Middle East?"

"Saturday afternoon. The day after the funeral."

"Do you have a cell phone? What number can we use if we need to speak with you again before you leave?"

"Umm, probably the best way will be to call Kristi. Either I'll be here or she'll know how to get a message to me."

"OK. Thanks, Mr. Meyers. And good-bye for now."

"Good-bye, detectives."

After hanging up, Ginny observed, "He sure seems to be close to and very concerned about the vic's widow."

"So I noticed. Either he's being a great friend to his dead buddy, or there's something more going on."

"Like what?"

"Like maybe he and the widow are more involved than we thought. Or at least Meyers would like to be a lot more involved. Heck, he sounds like he's already planned to spend his one-month leaves with the widow. If they are involved, that could give him, or her, or them a great motive for killing Dalton."

"Geez, Joe. You sure are cynical."

"I'm not saying that's what's going on, just that it's possible."

"I'll grant you that. But I don't see it. And I won't until or unless we get some evidence to support it."

"Fair enough. Not sure what I'm looking for, but I'm going to check with the junk-car rental companies in Columbus and try to find where Meyers rented the car when he and Dalton came to Ohio. The mileage, or maybe a parking ticket, might tell us more about their whereabouts when they were here."

"Go for it. Not sure it'll help, but it sure can't hurt."

"In any event, Ginny, I think we've run out of people to play that voicemail message to."

"We agree on that. And I'll bet you'll also agree with my next proposal."

"What's that?"

"That we head out and grab lunch."

"Now you're talking. Let's go."

Chapter 35

After their normal Tex-Mex lunch, Joe and Ginny were back at their desks. As they had agreed over lunch, Ginny called Sergeant James in Kansas City.

"Sergeant James here. How may I help you?"

"Good afternoon, Sergeant. This is your favorite pest, Detective Harris, back here in Ohio."

"Oh, hi, detective. Not to worry. You're not *that* big a pest. Just kidding. What's doing?"

"We've got a crazy hunch that we'd like you to try to run down for us."

"Happy to try to help. What's your crazy hunch?"

"We, in fact mostly Detective McFarland, wonder if there's something deeper than friendship going on between the victim's wife, or widow, and the victim's best friend, Alan Meyers. And, if there is, how long has it been going on for?"

"Aha. Do I smell a possible motive for murder here?"

"Well, it could be. And if it is, is the murderer him or her or both of them?"

"Wouldn't be the first time. Two great buddies, and buddy one is secretly in love with buddy two's wife or girlfriend. Maybe with the wife or girlfriend expressing the same feelings or maybe without her even realizing that buddy one is anything more than a good friend.

And, if there are those feelings, were they acted on while the victim was alive? Are they being acted on now?"

"Wow! Sergeant, you read way too many mystery and romance novels."

"Not me. I get my knowledge from TV shows. And, of course, the crazy real world we live in."

"Understood. Do you think you can check around a bit to see if there might be something that was or is going on?"

"Sure. Happy to. We'll keep an eye on Meyers while he's here in town and we'll talk with some of their mutual friends and former classmates."

"That would be great. Please be discreet so that neither Meyers nor the widow gets wise to what we're thinking and checking out."

"Will do. I'll get back to you in a couple of days. Friday, after the funeral, at the very latest."

"Great. We appreciate your help on this."

"No problem. Speak to you in a few. Bye."

"Good-bye, Sergeant. And thanks again."

"Well done, Ginny," said Joe. "Let's see what he comes up with."

"Yes. In the meantime, let's see if we can take a couple of good-sized bites out of the paperwork and actual detective work we have on our load of other cases."

"Sounds yummy. Let's do it."

Joe and Ginny remained focused on other cases until early Friday afternoon when Ginny's phone rang.

Chapter 36

"Hello. Detective Harris."

"Hi. This is your trusted assistant calling from your Kansas City branch office."

"Oh. Hi, Sergeant. How're you doing?"

"Just fine. Calling to report on our snooping in regard to your conspiracy theory."

"Well, I wouldn't call it that. But anyway, what did you find?"

"No smoking gun. But a few interesting tidbits."

"OK. Let's have 'em. I'm putting you on the speaker so Detective McFarland can hear this firsthand."

"Fine. Hello, detective."

"Hello, Sergeant. Whadda ya got?"

"Well, no smoking gun. But I think your wild hunch may be a little less wild than I first thought."

"Oh. Now you've got our interest," said Ginny.

"Yeah, I thought I might. We kept our eyes on Meyers the whole time he was here. In fact, that was rather easy to do. Except for trips to the supermarket and liquor store, one visit to his mother and, of course, the funeral, he never left the widow's house."

"You mean day and night?"

"Yup, exactly my point. Either there's some hanky-panky going on between those two, or he's one hell of a good friend."

"I'd say so," said Ginny. "Anything else?"

"Well, like I told you we would, Officer Jankowski and I attended the funeral. Rather than Meyers acting like a close friend of the vic and his widow, he and the widow spent the whole time together, greeting and thanking attendees for coming as if the two of them were a couple who suffered a family loss together."

"I get the picture," said Joe. "Anything else?"

"Nope. That's it. Nothing definitive, but it sort of gave me that itch under my skin, if you know what I mean."

"Sure do. We often get that same type of itch."

"Anything else you'd like me to do?"

"No. Nothing, at least for now. And many thanks for your help," said Joe.

"You're very welcome. Don't mention it. Just sorry I didn't find that smoking gun. What's your next move?"

"Good question," answered Ginny. "I think we need to speak with Meyers, hopefully in person, and maybe also the widow. Even if our suspicions are right, we still don't know if we're after him, her or them."

"Very intriguing. Keep me up to speed. And yell if I can do anything else to help."

"Will do. And thanks again. Bye."

"So long. You two take care."

After hanging up, Joe asked Ginny "OK, what exactly is our next step now?"

"Whatever it is, we'd better move fast. Meyers told us he's returning to Afghanistan the day after the funeral. If we want to talk to him, especially in person, we'd better get on it now."

"Right you are. Let's call Ann Messing to see if she can

get us the warrant we need to get him here to talk with us."

"On it."

"Hello. This is Assistant Prosecutor Ann Messing. How may I help you?"

"Hi, Ann. This is Ginny and Joe over at the PD in Jasper Creek."

"Hi, guys. What's cooking?"

"We've made some good progress on the Dalton murder and now we need your help."

"What can I do for you?"

Ginny described their suspicions, the report from Sergeant James, and Meyers' plan to return to Afghanistan. "We need you to prevent his leaving. In fact, we'd like him to be held and extradited to us here so we can interrogate him."

"Do you have any evidence beyond what you've told me?"

"We even checked out the car Meyers rented when he and Dalton arrived in Columbus to interview at Aegis. The rental company confirmed that he had it rented the entire time he was in Ohio and that he drove more than enough miles to have included a trip to Jasper Creek and back to Columbus."

"Is that it?" asked Messing.

"Yup. That's it so far," said Joe. "But there's a good chance we can get more, possibly even a confession, if we can talk with him."

"Well, unless he voluntarily wants to visit Jasper Creek, it ain't gonna happen. You have no real evidence on which to base a warrant for extradition. All you have is a hunch or, if you prefer, a theory. And you have no inkling whether his relationship with the widow is romantic or that of a good friend to the vic or who knows what."

"But if we don't do something, and quickly, he's out of the country tomorrow."

"Sorry. But that's the way it is. You know very well that warrants require evidence. Something you're sorely lacking so far."

"But …"

"Hey, you know I'd like to help, but without some significant evidence supporting probable cause, we can't do anything."

"Damn," said Joe. "That was directed at the situation, Ann, not at you."

"I know."

"OK. That's it for now, then. Thanks, Ann," said Ginny.

"Speak with both of you later."

"Bye."

"Bummer," said Joe. "Looks like he's gonna waltz right out of our clutches."

"Well, there's not much we can do about that. Let's move on. How about we have another discussion with the widow?"

"Sounds like a good next step. Let's see if Sergeant James can get her to his office. He can at least add a bit of seriousness to our discussion."

"Yeah. And he can also give us a read on her body language. I'll call him now."

Ginny called Sergeant James again and explained their request. James readily agreed and said he'd call Ginny back as soon as he spoke with Ms. Dalton. About an hour later, he called back and said that Ms. Dalton would be in his office at 9:30 Central time on Monday morning. Ginny thanked him and said they'd call his office on Monday.

With the weekend ahead of them, and both unable to forget the disappointing fact that there was no way they could stop Meyers from leaving the next day, Joe decided to suggest a different type of weekend to Ginny.

"OK, Ginny. It's time," said Joe.

"Time for what?"

"Let's head out of town for the weekend. Despite Meyers hightailing it back to Afghanistan, we've earned a reward for the progress we've made on the case. And we're both tired of having to hide inside all weekend."

"I can agree with that. But where are we going?"

"Trust me. I've got a good idea. I'll pick you up at 8 tomorrow morning. Pack only casual clothes, and include a bathing suit and good walking shoes."

"Is that all you're going to tell me?"

"Yup."

"OK, mystery man. I'm heading out now. I'll be packed and ready at eight tomorrow."

"Sounds like a plan. Have a good night."

"You too, Joe."

A few minutes later, Joe headed home. He called and made a reservation at the Lodge on Deer Creek, located in a state park about 30 minutes south of Columbus.

Chapter 37

Joe was parked outside Ginny's apartment at 7:45 the next morning, with a bag of Egg McMuffins and coffees for both of them. Ginny saw him through her window two minutes later, and came right out and got into Joe's car.

"Ready nice and early," said Joe. "I like that."

"Well, what did you expect? You're always early, so I'm ready for that."

"Appreciate it. One rule for this weekend. No, and I mean zero, discussion of the case. Or of any of our cases."

"Deal. Now can you tell me where we're going?"

"Nope. Just sit back and enjoy the journey."

About 90 minutes later, Joe drove into the state park and followed the signs to the lodge. When they arrived, Ginny was pleasantly surprised.

"Wow! This looks great, Joe. How'd you know about this place?"

"I came here a few times when I first moved to Jasper Creek. I still remember the quiet, pleasant surroundings, along with the various activities and meals available at the lodge. And, most important, we're pretty unlikely to bump into anyone we know."

"What a great surprise. Thanks."

Joe parked his car. They each grabbed their own bag and walked into the lobby. Joe led Ginny to the reception desk, where he referred to the reservation he had made and got them checked them in as Mr. and Mrs. McFarland. As the summer season had largely ended, Joe was able to get an oversized room with a view of the lake at no additional charge.

The weekend was more enjoyable than either of them had expected. They clearly needed some time totally devoid of police discussions and were long overdue for a weekend other than hiding in one of their houses. It was too cool to swim in the lake, but the hours flew by with swimming in and sitting at the heated swimming pool, renting a pontoon boat at the lakefront, soaking in the hot tub, hiking in the woods, a lot of eating and just sitting and talking. It was this last activity that was most special. Joe and Ginny felt that still more depth to their relationship had been reached, resulting in an even fuller sort of intimacy.

They joked, or half-joked, about being Mr. and Mrs. McFarland for the weekend. Several times, the conversations turned more serious. And, as the weekend progressed, they, especially Joe, became increasingly comfortable with discussing their feelings and their relationship.

"OK, Ginny. Let me try to summarize what we've been saying yesterday and this morning. I think it's pretty clear that we're in love and we're both enjoying life a lot more than we had been before. We also agree that we don't really know how this will develop and wind up. Marriage may or may not be in the cards, but it won't be tomorrow."

"Yes. And we have to add that we're both scared that this somehow won't work out, but there's not really anything we can do about it other than letting things evolve."

"Correct. And we also agreed that we'll keep all this quiet for the time being."

"Joe, I think you nailed the summary perfectly. How come you can't write up your notes at work half as well as this summary?"

"Hey, that's a low blow. Maybe it's 'cause I care more about this. And about you."

"Fair enough. Explanation accepted. Now, I'll race you into the pool and swimming to the other end."

Ginny jumped up and started racing to the pool. It took Joe a few seconds to realize what was happening, then he was right behind her.

Sunday afternoon came around much too soon for either of them. They checked out, drove back to Jasper Creek and spent the night at Joe's house.

Chapter 38

Monday morning, Joe dropped Ginny off at her apartment. She dropped off her suitcase and drove her own car to the PD.

Just before 10:30, Joe and Ginny went into the conference room. As she had agreed, Ginny placed a call to Sergeant James.

"Good morning. Sergeant James here at the KC PD. How may I help you?"

"Good morning, Sergeant. This is Detectives Harris and McFarland. How was your weekend?"

"Just fine. Thanks. And yours?"

"Couldn't have been better," answered Ginny. "Is Ms. Dalton with you?"

"Yes, she is. She arrived about 15 minutes ago. She's waiting in the conference room down the hall. Let me transfer this call there. I'll pick it up from there in a minute and we can then be on the speaker phone."

"Fine. And I'll put this on the speaker at our end as well."

After a couple of minutes' silence, "Hello. Can you hear me?"

"Yes, we can," said Ginny. "Good morning, Ms. Dalton. This is Detective Harris in Jasper Creek, Ohio, and Detective McFarland is here with me."

"Good morning, detectives."

"Thank you for going to Sergeant James' office. We

appreciate your help. Especially at what must be a very difficult time for you."

"You're welcome. I'm happy to help any way I can. But I'm not sure I can be of much help. And although this is a difficult time, it's not as bad as you might imagine. Even though we just had Paul's funeral, I really feel like I lost him a long time ago."

"Yes, you had mentioned that before. Nonetheless, did you have some people, relatives or friends, there with you for this tough period?"

"I did. I have my parents, of course. And also some good friends."

"That's good," said Ginny. "And did you see Alan Meyers much other than at the funeral?"

"Yes, some."

"Just some?" asked Joe.

"What do you mean?"

"It's my understanding that you and he were together almost constantly the whole time he was back home."

"Well, uh, he was best friends with Paul, you know."

"Yes, we do know that. We just hadn't realized what a dedicated friend he also is to you."

"What are you implying, detective?"

"Really just wondering. Not implying. Is your and Alan Meyers' relationship something more than he having been best friends with your husband?"

"Wow! You don't much beat around the bushes, do you?"

"Usually not."

"Well, I can assure you that from my viewpoint Alan is just a good friend. He was best friends with my husband,

and we became good friends as the three of us used to do everything together."

"And from Mr. Meyers' viewpoint?" asked Ginny.

"You'll have to ask Alan."

"Well, what do you think his viewpoint is?"

"To be honest, I'm not sure. I always had felt that his viewpoint was like mine. But this weekend was weird."

"Weird? How?" asked Joe.

"I'm not sure. He might have been acting just like a good friend, concerned about my feelings and the situation. Either as a friend to me or a friend to Paul. Or both. But I couldn't help feeling that he was also flirting with or coming on to me."

"Oh," said Ginny.

"I can't point to anything specific. It was more a feeling I had than anything specific he said or did."

"You two did spend virtually all the time he was home together. Even overnight," said Joe.

"Yeah, that was a bit weird. He didn't want to leave me alone. Even for a minute. But it's not like you make it sound. We slept in separate bedrooms and didn't do anything inappropriate."

"Well I'm certainly glad to hear that," said Joe. "Ms. Dalton, do you think Alan Meyers could have had anything to do with your husband's murder?"

"What? Of course not! He and Alan were best friends."

"Yes, but that doesn't always preclude murder. Could Meyers have been upset with your husband for how he treated you? Or was your husband being alive preventing Meyers from acting on his strong feelings for you?"

"No. I can't believe that of Alan."

"Well, we hope you're right. But for the time being, we have to keep him on our suspect list."

"I assume I'm on that list also. Even though I've never even been to Ohio in my life."

"Yes, technically you are also on the list," said Ginny. "But you're way down near the bottom of the list."

"Well, thank heaven for little things."

"Is there anything else you can tell us?" asked Joe.

"No, nothing I can think of."

"OK then. Thank you for your help, Ms. Dalton. We'll be back in touch if we have more questions or when we have more information for you. And, Sergeant, thanks for all your help. Good-bye now."

"Good-bye," said Sergeant James as he hung up.

"Well, that was rather illuminating," said Ginny.

"Yes, indeed. What's your take on it?"

"I think she had nothing to do with the murder. And I do think she was truly surprised by Meyers' apparent advances. But I can see several possible motives for Meyers to kill his best friend."

"Yeah. Love conquers all. Too bad we couldn't have kept him in the U.S."

"Joe, we need to figure out a way to get him back here. Right now, he's our hottest, and least accessible, suspect."

"Full agreement. We definitely have to get him back here. I can't quite picture the chief buying us two tickets to fly to Afghanistan."

"That'll be the day."

Chapter 39

Later that afternoon, Ginny had an idea. "Hey, Joe, this may sound too simple, but I think I know how to get Meyers back here."

"Even the chief says that simple is good. What's your idea?"

"What if we can get Aegis to bring him back to Columbus for some special training?"

"That's a great idea, Ginny. And we just happen to be there when he walks into the training room."

"Exactly. Let me call Captain Watkins and see if they'll do that for us. Patriotic spirit and all that stuff."

"Go for it."

So Ginny called Watkins.

"Nicole Watkins speaking. How may I help you?"

"Good afternoon, Captain. This is Detective Harris in Jasper Creek."

"Hello, detective. What can I do for you?"

"We need a little help. We have a favor to ask."

"Shoot. What is it?"

"As you know, Mr. Meyers has just returned to Afghanistan after attending his friend's funeral in Kansas City."

"Yes, that's correct. He landed there early this morning and will be back on assignment starting tomorrow."

"Yes. Well, we'd like your help in getting him back here."

"Huh? Why didn't you just ask him to stay while he was back in the States?"

"At the time, we weren't sure we needed him here. And we don't want to tip our hand prematurely."

"Do you think he's the murderer?"

"For now, let's just say that he's a person of interest. When is he next due back in the States?"

"Umm. Not for several months. Our normal tour, followed by a month's leave back in the U.S., is six months. And, as you know, he only started with us very recently."

"Yes, we know. How about bringing him back here for some special training?"

"But we have nothing …"

"Yes, we know there's no real special training here for him. But he doesn't need to know that."

"Oh, I see. I imagine we could do that. But I'd need to clear it with Colonel Burke first. He's the only one who could approve something like that."

"That would be fine. Just please make sure that Colonel Burke knows to keep this confidential."

"Will do. And no need to worry. We're always dealing with confidential info, so we know how to handle it."

"Great. Please check with the colonel and get back to me. And, if need be, Jasper Creek can reimburse your company for Meyers' airfare."

"OK. I'll talk to the colonel and get back to you after that."

"Great. Thanks for your help."

"You're welcome. Good-bye."

"Good-bye."

Chapter 40

Burke called Ginny around 10 o'clock the next morning.

"Good morning, detective. This is Colonel Burke at Aegis Control."

"Good morning, Colonel."

"Ms. Watkins told me about your request for us to help you get Mr. Meyers back here from Afghanistan. I'd like to get a few more details before I decide."

"Sure. No problem. Let me put you on the speaker. Detective McFarland is here with me."

"Good morning, Colonel."

"Good morning, detective."

"What would you like to know, Colonel?" asked Ginny.

"Well, before we agree to bring one of our employees back here on false pretenses, I'd like to understand why and how important it is. We sure run the risk of losing, or at a minimum demoralizing Meyers. And, depending on who else he tells, this could upset a number of our employees."

"Understood," said Ginny. "We wouldn't be asking if this weren't important. Right now, Meyers is our top suspect in the death of Paul Dalton. Unfortunately, we didn't come to this conclusion, based upon recently received information, until he was just about to leave the U.S. to return to Afghanistan. And, we didn't have enough evidence for a warrant to force him to remain in the U.S."

"Oh, OK. Is there any other way you can get him back here?"

"No," said Ginny. "This is the only chance we think we have."

"I see. That helps me better understand the situation. So, yes, despite the problems it may cause us, we'd be glad to help you out on this. And we can transport him back to the States on one of our cargo planes making the trip anyway, so there'll be no international airfare costs to worry about."

"Oh, that's wonderful. Thank you."

"I'll inform Ms. Watkins of our discussion and have her call you to work out the details."

"Thank you," said Joe and Ginny in unison.

"You're welcome. Good-bye."

"Good-bye."

Twenty minutes later, Watkins called Ginny. "Hello, detective. I just hung up with Colonel Burke. As you know, he's agreed to our helping you get Mr. Meyers back here. When do you want him here?"

"I suggest we wait a couple of weeks so that it doesn't seem too suspicious calling him back right after he left here."

"Understood. I can inform him around 10 days from now and then have him back here a few days after that."

"That sounds great. Please call me once you've informed him and you have an exact arrival date for him."

"OK. I'll do that. Bye for now."

"Good-bye. And thank you and the colonel again."

Ginny filled Joe in and then they both brought the chief and then Ann Messing in the Prosecutor's Office up to speed.

Joe and Ginny spent the next 10 days focused on other cases. They did, from time to time, talk about how they would deal with Meyers when they met with him in Columbus.

Chapter 41

Sure enough, 10 days later Watkins called Ginny.

"OK, detective. We're all set. I spoke with Meyers. He's all set to be back here next Tuesday morning to start his special training on differentiating friend from foe among the local population in Afghanistan."

"Great. That sounds like an important course. Too bad he won't be attending it."

"Yes. Well, we're not even offering that course now. Depending on how things develop between you and him, and between him and Aegis, he may or may not be able to take it sometime in the future."

"Very true. Did he seem at all suspicious?"

"No. Not at all. He seemed honored to have been chosen for the course."

"Great. Can you arrange for a private room where we can meet with him when he arrives?"

"Sure. He should get here about 8 a.m. on Tuesday."

"Super. We'll be there at least an hour earlier to get set up just in case he arrives early."

"OK. I'll get in early that day as well."

"Thank you for this."

"Don't mention it. We're happy to help. See you on Tuesday."

"Yup. See you then."

Joe and Ginny brought the chief up to speed and then went back to waiting for Tuesday to roll around.

Chapter 42

Tuesday morning, Joe picked Ginny up at 5:30, early enough to be sure they would get to Aegis well before Meyers. Even with their stopping at McDonald's for breakfast, driving to Columbus, parking and walking to Aegis' offices around the corner, they were in the reception area by 7:30 a.m. Five minutes later, as they had requested, they were joined by a Columbus PD detective.

"Good morning. I'm Detective Ginny Harris and this is Detective Joe McFarland. Thanks for meeting us so early."

"No problem. I'm usually up early anyhow. I'm Brian Daniels."

"Glad you're here," said Joe. "We think there's a good chance that the suspect, Alan Meyers, will voluntarily agree to come with us to Jasper Creek for questioning. But if not, it's good to have you here to prevent him from disappearing. We may need a few hours to try to get a warrant for extradition to Jasper Creek."

"Yeah. I know the drill. I've been on your side of these arrangements more times than I'd like to admit."

At that point, Watkins arrived. After introductions and hellos, she led the three detectives to a small conference room next to her office,

"I've arranged for the receptionist, who knows to act as if Meyers is one of several arriving for a course, to buzz the phone in here and then lead Meyers to this room.

She'll open the door, let him walk in and then close the door again. After that, he's all yours."

"Thank you again for all your help with this. We appreciate it," said Ginny.

"No problem. I'll be in my office next door if you need me." Watkins then left the room, closing the conference room door behind her.

The three detectives each took a seat around the small rectangular table and spent a few minutes just getting to know each other a little.

At 7:50, the phone buzzed once. About two minutes later, there was a soft knock on the door, which was immediately opened without waiting for a response to the knock. Meyers walked in and the door was shut behind him.

"Uh, what's this? Aren't you the two detectives I spoke with on the video phone about Paul Dalton's death?"

"Yes, that's correct. I'm Detective Harris. This is Detective McFarland, who was on the call with me. And this is Detective Daniels from the Columbus police department."

"Is this about Paul's murder? Can we do this later today? I came here from Afghanistan for special training and the course is about to begin."

"That's all right, Mr. Meyers. Please take a seat. Captain Watkins said it would be OK if we took care of this first."

"OK," said Meyers as he sat down. "Do you have some news? Or do you have more questions for me?"

"Some of each," said Joe. "But mostly questions for you."

"OK. Ask away."

"First we need to read you the Miranda warning."

"What? Why? Do you think I'm the murderer?"

"Not sure yet. So I'll read you the warning just to be safe."

Joe pulled out the well-worn card from his wallet and read the warning.

"Yeah, sure. I understand what you just read. But I'm happy to talk with you. I want to do everything I can to help you solve Paul's murder."

"Before we proceed, we'd rather we all go back to our offices in Jasper Creek."

"What? Why? How long will this take?"

"Well, as you know, Jasper Creek is where Paul was killed. And we have certain things there that we want to show you."

"But what about my course here? I don't want to miss that much. And I don't have a car. How'll I get back here?"

"Not to worry. That'll all be taken care of. Mr. Meyers, you have two choices. Number one, and the better choice, is to voluntarily come with us to Jasper Creek. Number two, if you don't choose number one, involves Detective Daniels holding you at his precinct in Columbus until we get a warrant authorizing your extradition to Jasper Creek. So, either way, you'll be with us in Jasper Creek. It's your choice whether it's fast and friendly or drawn out and less than friendly."

"Are you saying I'm actually a suspect in Paul's death?"

"That's precisely why we want you to come with us and talk with us. After that, I'm sure we can better answer that question."

"Well, given the two choices, it's pretty clear which one makes sense. Let's go. But can I first tell Captain Watkins what's going on and why I'll be missing the start of the class?"

"Smart decision, Mr. Meyers. And Ms. Watkins is already aware of all this. Let's get started."

A quick good-bye and thanks to Detective Daniels, and Joe, Ginny and Meyers were quickly in Joe's car, heading to Jasper Creek.

Chapter 43

With Meyers locked in one of the small interrogation rooms at PD headquarters, Ginny called Ann Messing, bringing her up to speed on the investigation and inviting her to come over and witness Meyers' interrogation. While waiting for Messing to arrive, Joe and Ginny brought the chief up to date.

"Nice. Looks like you two super sleuths have made some good progress. Let's hope the next step is a solved case."

"We're hoping right alongside you, Chief," said Joe. "But let's not celebrate prematurely."

"Understood. Now it would be nice if you got a nice clean confession from your suspect. Then we can celebrate."

"We'll do the best we can, Chief."

"I know you two will. Go get 'em."

"On our way," said Ginny as she and Joe left the chief's office and went back to their desks to wait for Messing to arrive.

Ten minutes later, after reassuring Messing that they had properly Mirandized Meyers, Messing was standing outside the one-way window looking into the interrogation room. Joe and Ginny walked into the interrogation room, carrying three coffees and several files. They sat down across from Meyers.

"Here's a coffee for you if you wish," said Joe. "It tastes lousy, but it's hot and strong."

"Thanks."

"Mr. Meyers, we're going to record this. For both our protections."

"OK."

"Let's get started." Joe turned on the recorder and stated the date, the names of the three people in the room and the date and time that he had read his Miranda rights to Meyers.

Joe, with some assistance from Ginny, spent about the first half hour questioning Meyers about his relationship with Paul, from grade school up to the present.

"And what about Kristi Dalton?"

"What about her?"

"Where did she fit in with the relationship between you and Paul?"

"Early on, like in grade school, Kristi was the typical tomboy. She was in school with us so we, of course, knew her. She sometimes joined us for hikes or sports, but there was nothing special in our relationships back then."

"And then?" asked Ginny.

"In high school, she and Paul started dating. And soon it got pretty serious. They were going steady and spending most of their free time together."

"And what about you?"

"Well. The three of us often spent time together and did things together. But, naturally, there were also times when just the two of them did stuff and went places together."

"And how did that make you feel?"

"What do you mean?"

"Did you feel left out? Or like the third wheel when you were all together?"

"No. Of course not. I was real happy for them. Being in love and all."

"That's not what we heard," said Ginny.

"What did you hear?"

"That you put up a good front, but you were really upset. And hurt. And jealous."

"Whoever told you that is full of it. I was real happy for Paul and Kristi."

"Well, let's agree to disagree on that for now," said Joe. "And how about when they got married?"

"I was thrilled for them. Hell, I was Paul's best man at the wedding."

"Yeah," said Joe. "And wishing he were the best man while you were marrying Kristi."

"No way. I see what you're implying, but you're wrong."

"What do you think I'm implying?" asked Joe.

"That I was secretly in love with Kristi. And jealous of Paul for her marrying him. And that somehow that's the motive for why I killed him."

"Boy. I couldn't have said it any better," said Joe.

"This is crazy. You have this crazy theory. But with no evidence to support it."

"We'll talk about our evidence later. Tell us how you felt after Paul left the service, when he started having trouble adjusting to civilian life. And how he mistreated his family and finally walked out on Kristi."

"He was a real shit. Kristi didn't deserve any of that. She's a great person. She tried to help Paul all she could, and he just dumped all over her. He wrote her a damn two-sentence note and left. No explanation. No money. No nothing."

"What did you do during all that?" asked Ginny.

"I tried. Believe me, I tried. I can't tell you how many discussions, and, yeah, sometimes arguments, Paul and I had. But he had changed overseas. He wasn't the same Paul when he came back. I couldn't get him to change, or even try to change, anything."

"And Kristi?"

"She and I talked a lot. I kept trying to cheer her up. I'd tell her what I was going to talk to Paul about and how things would get better. God, I would have done anything to make things better for Kristi."

"Anything?" asked Ginny.

"Well, almost anything. Not murdering Paul, if that's what you mean."

"So you and Kristi were often together, sneaking around behind Paul's back?"

"Yes. But not the way you're implying. We didn't do anything wrong. We only talked. About getting Paul to change and making things better for Paul. And for Kristi."

"I bet you were wishing that you and Kristi were doing more than just talking," said Joe.

"No. Well, yeah. That's true. I guess I actually loved Kristi without even realizing it. But I wouldn't do, or try, anything funny. She was married to my best friend."

"Yes," said Joe. "The girl you loved was married to your best friend, and your best friend was making her life miserable."

"OK. Yeah, I loved, and I love Kristi. But that's not a crime."

"That's true. Let's talk about how you and she spent the whole time around Paul's funeral playing house."

"What do you mean?"

"Except for one brief visit to your mother and a few trips to the supermarket, you never left Kristi's house. Day or night."

"That's not what you think. I was trying to make her feel better and have some hope. We weren't having sex or anything like that."

"So you say. But it sure looks suspicious."

"Just because I loved Kristi? Hell, I think I loved her before Paul did. I was just always too chicken to say or do anything about it. But loving her isn't a crime."

"No it isn't. But killing someone because of it is."

"You can't prove that. You have no evidence. Just your crazy theory."

"Excuse us. Detective Harris, can you join me outside for a minute?"

"Sure."

Joe and Ginny walked out of the room and joined Messing.

"OK, I think it's fibbing time," said Joe.

"Whadda ya have in mind?" asked Ginny.

"I think we should tell him that voice recognition software identified him as the one who left that voicemail message on Dalton's phone."

"But what if it wasn't him, and he calls your bluff?" asked Messing.

"My gut tells me it was him. In any event, we don't have much else. This might be what we need to push him into confessing."

"I agree with you, Joe. Let's go for it."

"OK, then," said Messing.

"Joe and Ginny walked back into the interrogation room.

"Now where were we?" asked Joe.

"Mr. Meyers was saying we had no evidence, just a crazy theory," said Ginny.

"Oh, yes, I remember. Are you sure, Mr. Meyers? Let's talk about Sergeant Andrews."

"Sergeant Andrews?"

"You remember. We played you that recording from Mr. Dalton's cell phone telling him not to return to Aegis, but to go to a certain location in Columbus to meet Colonel Burke."

"Yes. And I didn't recognize his voice."

"No one did. But thank heaven for modern technology."

"Huh? What do you mean?"

"Well, with the help of technology from the Ohio BCI — that's the Ohio Bureau of Criminal Investigation, sort of like our state-level FBI — we were able to unmask the disguised voice and match the voice of the caller who left that message. And you, Mr. Meyers, have been identified as the voice of the mysterious Sergeant Andrews."

"That's ridiculous. And anyhow, I was always with Paul around the time of that call. So how could I have done it?"

"Not yet sure if you or he stepped into the bathroom for a few minutes. Or if one of you took a brief walk outside. Or went out to buy some food. In any event, that recorded voice is your voice."

"OK. I'd like to get a lawyer now."

"That's probably a good idea. We'll have to hold you in a cell until the public defender can assign someone. Unless you have or want to hire a private lawyer."

"A public defender is fine."

"No problem. Just be aware that the Prosecutor's Office will be much less likely to consider a plea bargain, where you plead guilty in exchange for a reduced sentence, once you have a lawyer."

"Uh, wait. Let me think about this for a few minutes."

"OK, Mr. Meyers. We'll step outside for a few minutes. You can tell us what you've decided when we come back."

Joe and Ginny walked out and joined Messing.

"Good work, guys. You're close to getting his confession."

"Yeah, unless he lawyers up," said Joe.

"Your little fib about the voice on that recorded message seemed to have hit the nail on the head."

"Yeah. Even we get lucky occasionally," said Ginny. "And it was a lie for a very good cause."

"What can we offer him in exchange for a confession?" asked Joe.

"I discussed this with my boss before I came over. In exchange for his confession, we would lower the charge from aggravated murder to murder. That would lower his prison time from anywhere between 25 years and life to probably 15 to 25 years. And possibly less with the chance of parole."

"That's a pretty good deal," said Ginny. "But let's first get the chief on board in case Meyers goes for it."

"OK, Ginny. Why don't you go see the chief? While

you're doing that, I'll get someone to run out and get some lunch for all of us."

"Sounds like a plan."

Chapter 44

Joe and Ginny walked back into the interrogation room. They had given one sandwich to Messing and carried the other three in with them.

"Tuna or ham and cheese?" asked Ginny.

"What?"

"We've got sandwiches for lunch. Do you want a tuna or a ham and cheese sandwich?"

"Uh. Ham and cheese, please. And thanks."

"OK. And someone will be bringing in fresh coffee for us. So, Mr. Meyers, have you decided about wanting a lawyer now?"

"Sort of. Can you give me some idea of how much the prison sentence would be reduced if I confess? And how can I be sure I can believe you?"

"Two good questions, Mr. Meyers. Shows you've been thinking. The assistant prosecutor who is assigned your case is outside. Let me invite her in and you can hear it from the horse's mouth."

Joe stepped out and returned with Messing right behind him. He made the introductions, after which he and Messing sat down.

"Mr. Meyers," said Messing, "Detective McFarland told me your two questions. I can answer both of them for you. First of all, you have my word as a member of the Prosecutor's Office, and this is being recorded, that in exchange for your full confession, we will reduce the charge from aggravated murder to murder. You will have to make a written confession now, and then confess orally in court. Judges are not required to follow our sentencing recommendations, but they almost always do. Rather than 25 years to life, you'd most likely serve 15 to 25 years, and maybe less with the possibility of parole."

"Uh, let me just think for a couple of minutes."

"Sure," said Joe. "We'll be outside the window over there. Just wave when you're ready and we'll come back in."

And with that, Joe, Ginny and Messing walked out.

Less than five minutes later, Meyers waved. Joe, Ginny and Messing were quickly back in their seats in the interrogation room.

"OK. I'll agree to confess based on the terms you explained to me."

"A wise choice," said Messing. I'll leave you and the two detectives to get your written confession, including your explaining some of the details we haven't yet figured out. After that, you'll be arrested, a public defender will be assigned your case and we'll move to get this on the court calendar as quickly as we can. Good-bye, Mr. Meyers."

"Good-bye."

Joe and Ginny then spent the next two hours getting Meyers to make a full confession, orally and in writing. They asked many questions so that they could close the numerous gaps in their knowledge about all the details of the murder. Following that, Meyers was arrested, photographed, fingerprinted and locked in a cell.

With a written confession and plea bargain agreed to

by Messing and Meyers, things proceeded rapidly. The court hearing was scheduled for the following Monday morning.

Chapter 45

"**C**ome on, Joe. Let's get over to the courthouse. Meyers' hearing will be starting soon."

"OK. Let's go. I don't want to miss this."

"Nice to have this wrapped up so quickly. Without a confession and plea deal, these trials get delayed for mega months."

"No question about it. It's also nice that we'll just be sitting in the back as spectators. We don't even have to testify."

"Yup. It's a three-person show, starring the judge, Meyers and Messing. Well, three and a half if you include Meyers' public defender."

Joe and Ginny were seated in the last row of a packed courtroom.

The whole court hearing took less than 20 minutes.

"Court is now in session, the Honorable Judge Richard Erwin presiding."

"Mr. Meyers, your counsel has informed the court that you told him you decided to proceed without a lawyer. Is that correct?"

"Yes, it is, your honor."

"So, Mr. Meyers, have you definitely decided to waive your right to counsel? And do you understand what waiving that right means?"

"Yes, your Honor."

"Counsel, have you reached a settlement?" asked the judge as he looked at Messing.

"Your Honor, we and the defendant have agreed upon a plea deal which we believe is fair to both sides."

"Let's hear it."

"Yes, your Honor. In exchange for his confession to murder in the second degree, we have agreed to recommend a prison term of 15 to 25 years, with the possibility of parole before that."

"Mr. Meyers, do you know that by pleading guilty you lose the right to a jury trial? And do you give up that right?" asked the judge.

"Yes, your Honor, I do."

"Do you understand what giving up that right means?" asked the judge.

"Yes."

"Do you know that you are waiving the right to cross-examine your accusers?"

"Yes."

"And do you know that you are waiving your privilege against self-incrimination?"

"Yes."

"Did anyone force you into accepting this settlement?"

"No."

"OK, then. In the matter of the *State vs. Meyers,* Mr. Meyers, how do you plead?" asked the judge.

"Guilty, your Honor."

"Are you pleading guilty because you did in fact shoot and kill the victim without legal provocation?"

"Yes."

"We need you to state that now, Mr. Meyers."

"OK. I am pleading guilty because I did shoot and kill the victim without legal provocation."

"Thank you. Mr. Meyers, you are hereby found guilty of murder in the second degree and sentenced to a prison term of 23 years in the Ohio State Penitentiary in Youngstown, with the possibility of earlier parole. Does anyone have anything else?" asked the judge.

After a few minutes of silence, the judge continued, "Bailiff, please remove the prisoner. Court adjourned."

Messing walked back to the PD with Joe and Ginny. The chief joined the three of them in the conference room for a celebratory cup of stale coffee.

"Congratulations. You two did a great job of sleuthing, and with Ann's help, got a super confession. And as they say, 'the rest is history.' "

"Yes," added Messing. "The prosecutor, and I'm sure the town's political brass, are delighted to have this behind us."

"Yeah," said Joe. "And without the long delay of waiting for a trial, with who knows what outcome."

"Amen to that," said Messing.

"And I'm glad how you two also answered all the minor but annoying open questions," said the chief. "Like how Meyers used his rental car to pick Dalton up on that street corner in Columbus and drive him here."

"Yeah," said Joe. "And swinging by the Scioto River along the way back to dump his gun."

"Dalton sure must have been surprised when he was met on that street corner by Meyers rather than Colonel Burke," said Ginny.

"Yeah," said Joe, "but Meyers was pretty sharp in

explaining to Dalton that it, as well as their visit to the warehouse, was all part of Aegis' testing and training program for them."

"No question," said Joe. "These recruits would believe just about anything about Burke and Aegis. The more mysterious and secret, the more believable it probably was."

"Speaking of believable, Ann, where are you guys with Watkins and Pentell's embezzlement scheme with the rental of that office here?"

"Funny you should ask. That just got resolved today. We're not going to pursue prosecution."

"Huh? Why not?" asked Joe.

"First of all, it might be difficult to prove embezzlement rather than stupid or poor negotiating. But more to the point, the colonel said that neither he nor Aegis would file a complaint. They agreed to drop everything in exchange for Watkins resigning from Aegis, and forfeiting her deferred bonus, and Pentell reimbursing Aegis for the excess rent and agreeing to immediately cancel the lease."

"That seems reasonable," said Ginny.

"Oh, and Watkins mentioned to me that she and Pentell are planning to move to Florida as soon as Pentell's divorce is final."

"Makes sense to me," said the chief. "Warm, sunny weather beats a cold, dark prison cell any day of the week in my book."

"Well said, Chief," said Ginny.

"The only thing I still have to do is make a few calls to Kansas City. I want to bring the widow up to date. This whole thing has to be rough for her, even with her prior separation from the vic."

"Yeah, a little closure for her would be nice," said Joe.

"Yes, it would. And I promised Sergeant James that we'd keep him informed."

"Go for it. And then it's time for lunch. You guys are more than welcome to join us," said Joe.

Both Messing and the chief thanked Joe but declined the lunch invitation.

Ginny called Sergeant James and brought him up to date. He congratulated Ginny and thanked her for the update. He finished by inviting her and Joe back to Kansas City anytime they'd like and stating that he might surprise them by showing up in Ohio one of these days.

Ginny then made her other call.

"Hello."

"Hello. Is this Ms. Dalton?"

"Yes, it is. Who is this?"

"Mrs. Dalton, this is Detective Harris from Jasper Creek, Ohio."

"Oh, hi. Sorry, but I didn't recognize your voice."

"That's quite all right. I'm calling to fill you in on the latest events."

"Oh, OK. What's going on?"

"Mrs. Dalton, it turns out that your husband was killed by Alan Meyers."

"What? No, that can't be. He and Paul were best friends. Forever."

"I'm sorry, but it is true. He made a full confession."

"My god. Why would he kill Paul?"

"Mrs. Dalton, it turns out that he did it because of you."

"What?"

"I'm afraid that you were indirectly his motive. He apparently was silently in love with you for years. But he wouldn't say or do anything because Paul was his best friend."

"I can't believe it. I had no idea. I thought we were just good friends. Although this does reinforce the weird feelings I had when he was here for the funeral. I guess his coming on to me was real, not just my imagination. But I can't believe he would have killed Paul because of me."

"We know that you had no idea until the days around the funeral. He was secretly in love with you for years, as far back as high school. But somehow over time he became obsessed with you. He became very upset with your husband about how he was treating you once he left the Army. And how he ran out on you. He thought he could be with you if only he could get your husband completely out of the way."

"My God. This is mind-boggling. All those years, I never had any idea. And I don't think I ever did or said anything to lead him to believe that I …"

"No, Mrs. Dalton. We know you didn't. Please don't in any way blame yourself for this. Blame falls 100% on Mr. Meyers. No one else bears any fault for your husband's murder."

"What happens now?"

"Just a few minutes ago, Mr. Meyers was sentenced to 23 years in prison in Ohio. He might get out on parole sometime sooner, but it will be quite a while."

"What a mess."

"Yes, it is. But murder usually causes a mess. Will you be OK?"

"Yes, or at least I think so. Luckily, my parents live nearby and they've been a godsend. Oh, I have to go see Mrs. Meyers. She must be heartbroken."

"Yes, I'm sure she is. She was here at the court hearing. She'll probably be home in a few days. I don't know if she'll stay out there or move to Ohio to be close to her son. What a shame."

"Oh, I feel so bad for her. Detective, thank you for calling to give me the news."

"You're very welcome. And the best of luck to you. Good-bye."

"Thank you. Good-bye."

As soon as Ginny hung up, Joe could see that Ginny was upset. "Ginny, you OK?"

"Yeah. I just feel bad for the widow. She's had a lot dumped on her."

"Yes she has. By her husband and his best friend. Hey, I've got a great idea," said Joe.

"This I gotta hear."

"How about we drive over to the mall and have some barbecue for lunch. It's not the greatest barbecue like we had in Kansas City, but it's more appropriate than tacos for celebrating closure of this case."

"Great idea, Joe. We also need to continue our discussion about us."

"Yeah, I knew that was coming. But you're right."

With a pulled pork sandwich and Diet Coke for Ginny and the three-meat combo plate and a Diet Coke for Joe, they grabbed an empty table in the back corner of the restaurant.

"Joe, it's a good thing that your diet didn't last too long."

"Well, you convinced me that I was already in good shape. Plus, this is mostly protein and you can't go wrong with that."

"If you say so. But seriously, Joe, what are we going to do about us?"

"That's a hell of a good question. I love being with you, and I'm pretty sure you feel the same way."

"You know I do."

"Yeah, but we're both getting tired of having to sneak around, holing up in your apartment or my house."

"Or driving more than an hour away to have dinner in a restaurant."

"I know it's tough, Ginny. But with the chief being as unpredictable as he is, we don't want to have him put an end to our partnership."

"Or even make one of us leave the department."

"Ouch."

"So what do we do, Joe? We can continue our sneaking around for a little while longer, but neither of us wants to live this way indefinitely."

"You got that right. But as super detectives, we should be able to come up with a solution."

"You would think so."

"Tell you what. Let's continue as is for now, but give ourselves 90 days to come up with a solution."

"And what if we don't come up with a solution in 90 days?"

"That, my dear, has to be answered as part of the solution or non-solution we come up with."

"OK. Fair enough, Joe. But only on one condition."

"What's that?"

"That this is not just a way of sticking our heads in the sand for 90 days. We have to commit to discussing this, in detail, at least twice a week."

"I can live with that."

"Deal?" asked Ginny.

"Deal," said Joe. "Now let's dig into our barbecue before it gets ice cold."

"Roger that, detective."

Born in Brooklyn, NY, Stuart has lived in 7 states and 4 European countries. He and his wife now live in the foothills of the Blue Ridge Mountains. Stuart earned an engineering degree from Swarthmore College and an MBA from Harvard University. His career has included work for large multinational firms, small startups and management consulting firms. Stuart and his wife are instrument-rated private pilots and Stuart is a volunteer firefighter & EMT and a Red Cross Disaster Responder.

See what Stuart Safft is up to at his blog: https://stuartsafft.wordpress.com.

Other Books from Stuart Safft

Where's Ellen?
A Joe McFarland / Ginny Harris Mystery

www.ingramcontent.com/pod-product-compliance
Lightning Source LLC
Chambersburg PA
CBHW021340290326
41933CB00037B/240